TOP NINJA AIR FRYER

Cookbook 2023

| 1600 | Days Crispy & Guilt-free Recipes Book for beginners to Cooking Made Effortless, Eating Made Healthier |

Latasha D. Hegarty

CONTENTS

Poultry Recipes *23*

Beef & Lamb And Pork Recipes *34*

Fish & Seafood Recipes 43

INTRODUCTION

Welcome, dear reader, to a tantalizing tale spun in the heart of your kitchen. But this isn't any ordinary tale. It's the tale of how a clever little machine called an air fryer met a visionary chef named Latasha D. Hegarty, and together, they embarked on a mission to transform the way we cook and eat.

Latasha isn't just a chef; she's an alchemist of flavor, a maestro of crunch, and a champion of health. When she first discovered the air fryer, she recognized not just an appliance, but a culinary game-changer. With a flash of inspiration and a dash of trial and error, she set out to harness its power for maximum flavor, minimal oil, and a tantalizing array of dishes that dance on the palate and nourish the body.

As you turn the pages of this cookbook, imagine you're stepping into Latasha's kitchen. You're there beside her as she stirs, seasons, and most importantly, explores. Each recipe is an adventure, an experiment where hot air and bold flavors combine to create something spectacular. From crispy appetizers to succulent main courses and decadent desserts, you'll journey through a variety of dishes that highlight the sheer versatility and potential of air frying.

This cookbook is more than just a guide—it's a ticket to a culinary journey, curated by Latasha D. Hegarty. As you embark on this voyage, let the aromas fill your kitchen, let the flavors enthrall your taste buds, and most importantly, let the joy of cooking with an air fryer inspire you, one delectable dish at a time.

Welcome aboard, culinary explorers. Your adventure begins here.

Ten Reasons to Love Air Fryer Cookbook

Healthier Meals

Air Fryer cookbooks provide recipes that require significantly less oil compared to traditional frying methods, which means lower fat and calorie intake.

Variety

A good Air Fryer Cookbook introduces a vast range of recipes, from appetizers to main courses and even desserts, showcasing the versatility of the appliance.

Easy-to-Follow Instructions

Clear, step-by-step instructions make cooking with an Air Fryer approachable for both beginners and seasoned cooks.

Saves Time

Many recipes in the Air Fryer Cookbook can be prepared in a fraction of the time it takes for conventional cooking methods, perfect for busy lifestyles.

Less Mess

Cooking with an Air Fryer often means fewer dishes and less splattering oil, and the cookbook offers tips to ensure a tidy kitchen post-cooking.

Ingredient Insights

The cookbook offers guidance on the best ingredients to use for optimal flavor and texture when air frying.

Taste and Texture

The recipes are tailored to achieve a crispy exterior and juicy interior, proving that healthier doesn't have to compromise on taste.

Innovative Ideas

A well-curated Air Fryer Cookbook offers fresh and innovative meal ideas, breaking the monotony of typical meals.

Budget-Friendly

Many recipes make use of everyday pantry staples, ensuring delicious meals without breaking the bank.

Enhances Appliance Utility

With a comprehensive cookbook, users can truly maximize the potential of their Air Fryer, making it an indispensable kitchen gadget.

Remember, an Air Fryer Cookbook isn't just a compilation of recipes; it's a guide that empowers users to cook efficiently and healthily, while enjoying delicious meals.

Is an Air Fryer good for people's health?

An Air Fryer offers several health benefits, primarily through its alternative cooking method which minimizes the use of oils and fats. Here are some of the specific health benefits associated with using an Air Fryer:

• Reduced Fat Intake

Traditional frying methods immerse food in oil, leading to a significant increase in fat content. In contrast, air frying uses up to 70-80% less oil, resulting in dishes with a considerably lower fat content.

• Lower Calorie Consumption

Due to the reduced oil usage, the calorie content of air-fried dishes is often lower than their traditionally fried counterparts. Over time, this can support weight management efforts.

• Decreased Risk of Toxic Compounds

Traditional frying can lead to the formation of harmful compounds like acrylamide, which is linked to adverse health effects. Air frying reduces the formation of such compounds.

• Less Trans Fats

Store-bought fried foods often contain trans fats, which are linked to increased risks of heart disease, stroke, and type 2 diabetes. Preparing meals at home with an Air Fryer eliminates the intake of these harmful trans fats.

• Supports a Balanced Diet

Air Fryers can also be used to cook a variety of vegetables and proteins without the excess oil, making it easier to maintain a balanced and varied diet.

• Reduced Inflammatory Effects

Consuming large amounts of fried foods can increase inflammation in the body. By minimizing the oil content in meals, Air Fryers can help reduce the inflammatory effects associated with excessive oil consumption.

• Heart Health

As Air Fryers can reduce the intake of unhealthy fats and harmful compounds, they can indirectly support heart health when used as part of a balanced diet.

Q&A about Air Fryers

Q: How much oil do I need to use in an Air Fryer?

A: Most Air Fryer recipes require little to no oil. Typically, you might use a tablespoon or even just a spray to coat the food, ensuring it gets a crispy exterior.

Q: Can I cook frozen foods in an Air Fryer?

A: Absolutely! Frozen foods can be cooked directly in an Air Fryer without thawing. However, you may need to adjust the cooking time and temperature.

Q: How do I clean my Air Fryer?

A: After the Air Fryer cools down, remove the basket and pan. Most Air Fryers have dishwasher-safe parts. If washing by hand, use warm soapy water and a non-abrasive sponge. Don't forget to wipe down the interior with a damp cloth occasionally.

Q: Is preheating necessary before cooking with an Air Fryer?

A: While many recipes might not require preheating, doing so can help achieve more consistent and faster cooking results. It usually takes 2-5 minutes to preheat.

Q: Can I use aluminum foil or baking paper in an Air Fryer?

A: Yes, but ensure that they don't obstruct the air circulation. Always place them in such a way that they're weighed down by food to prevent them from getting sucked into the heater.

Q: Is it possible to overfill or overcrowd the Air Fryer basket?

A: Yes, for optimal cooking and crisping, it's essential not to overcrowd the basket. Overfilling can impede airflow and result in unevenly cooked food.

Q: Why is my air-fried food not crispy?

A: This can result from overcrowding the basket or not using a small amount of oil. Spritzing food with a bit of oil can enhance its crispiness.

Q: Can I stack or layer food in an Air Fryer?

A: While some foods might be okay to stack, it's generally recommended to arrange them in a single layer for even cooking. If you must stack, ensure you frequently shake or rotate for uniform cooking.

Q: Is it normal for an Air Fryer to produce smoke?

A: While a little smoke is normal, excessive smoke could indicate a buildup of oil or food residues at the bottom. Regular cleaning can prevent this.

Measurement Conversions

BASIC KITCHEN CONVERSIONS & EQUIVALENTS

DRY MEASUREMENTS CONVERSION CHART

3 TEASPOONS = 1 TABLESPOON = 1/16 CUP

6 TEASPOONS = 2 TABLESPOONS = 1/8 CUP

12 TEASPOONS = 4 TABLESPOONS = 1/4 CUP

24 TEASPOONS = 8 TABLESPOONS = 1/2 CUP

36 TEASPOONS = 12 TABLESPOONS = 3/4 CUP

48 TEASPOONS = 16 TABLESPOONS = 1 CUP

METRIC TO US COOKING CONVERSIONS

OVEN TEMPERATURES

120 °C = 250 °F

160 °C = 320 °F

180° C = 350 °F

205 °C = 400 °F

220 °C = 425 °F

LIQUID MEASUREMENTS CONVERSION CHART

8 FLUID OUNCES = 1 CUP = 1/2 PINT = 1/4 QUART

16 FLUID OUNCES = 2 CUPS = 1 PINT = 1/2 QUART

32 FLUID OUNCES = 4 CUPS = 2 PINTS = 1 QUART

 = 1/4 GALLON

128 FLUID OUNCES = 16 CUPS = 8 PINTS = 4 QUARTS = 1 GALLON

BAKING IN GRAMS

1 CUP FLOUR = 140 GRAMS

1 CUP SUGAR = 150 GRAMS

1 CUP POWDERED SUGAR = 160 GRAMS

1 CUP HEAVY CREAM = 235 GRAMS

VOLUME

1 MILLILITER = 1/5 TEASPOON

5 ML = 1 TEASPOON

15 ML = 1 TABLESPOON

240 ML = 1 CUP OR 8 FLUID OUNCES

1 LITER = 34 FL. OUNCES

WEIGHT

1 GRAM = .035 OUNCES

100 GRAMS = 3.5 OUNCES

500 GRAMS = 1.1 POUNDS

1 KILOGRAM = 35 OUNCES

US TO METRIC COOKING CONVERSIONS

1/5 TSP = 1 ML

1 TSP = 5 ML

1 TBSP = 15 ML

1 FL OUNCE = 30 ML

1 CUP = 237 ML

1 PINT (2 CUPS) = 473 ML

1 QUART (4 CUPS) = .95 LITER

1 GALLON (16 CUPS) = 3.8 LITERS

1 OZ = 28 GRAMS

1 POUND = 454 GRAMS

BUTTER

1 CUP BUTTER = 2 STICKS = 8 OUNCES = 230 GRAMS = 8 TABLESPOONS

WHAT DOES 1 CUP EQUAL

1 CUP = 8 FLUID OUNCES

1 CUP = 16 TABLESPOONS

1 CUP = 48 TEASPOONS

1 CUP = 1/2 PINT

1 CUP = 1/4 QUART

1 CUP = 1/16 GALLON

1 CUP = 240 ML

BAKING PAN CONVERSIONS

1 CUP ALL-PURPOSE FLOUR = 4.5 OZ

1 CUP ROLLED OATS = 3 OZ 1 LARGE EGG = 1.7 OZ

1 CUP BUTTER = 8 OZ 1 CUP MILK = 8 OZ

1 CUP HEAVY CREAM = 8.4 OZ

1 CUP GRANULATED SUGAR = 7.1 OZ

1 CUP PACKED BROWN SUGAR = 7.75 OZ

1 CUP VEGETABLE OIL = 7.7 OZ

1 CUP UNSIFTED POWDERED SUGAR = 4.4 OZ

BAKING PAN CONVERSIONS

9-INCH ROUND CAKE PAN = 12 CUPS

10-INCH TUBE PAN =16 CUPS

11-INCH BUNDT PAN = 12 CUPS

9-INCH SPRINGFORM PAN = 10 CUPS

9 X 5 INCH LOAF PAN = 8 CUPS

9-INCH SQUARE PAN = 8 CUPS

Breakfast & Snacks And Fries Recipes

Polenta Fries

Servings: 6
Cooking Time:xx
Ingredients:

- 800 ml/scant 3½ cups water
- 1½ vegetable stock cubes
- ¾ teaspoon dried oregano
- ¾ teaspoon freshly ground black pepper
- 200 g/1⅓ cups quick-cook polenta/cornmeal
- 2 teaspoons olive oil
- 55 g/6 tablespoons plain/all-purpose flour (gluten-free if you wish)
- garlic mayonnaise, to serve

Directions:

1. Bring the water and stock cubes to the boil in a saucepan with the oregano and black pepper. Stir in the polenta/cornmeal and continue to stir until the mixture becomes significantly more solid and is hard to stir – this should take about 5–6 minutes.
2. Grease a 15 x 15-cm/6 x 6-in. baking pan with some of the olive oil. Tip the polenta into the baking pan, smoothing down with the back of a wet spoon. Leave to cool at room temperature for about 30 minutes, then pop into the fridge for at least an hour.
3. Remove the polenta from the fridge and carefully tip out onto a chopping board. Slice the polenta into fingers 7.5 x 1 x 2 cm/3 x ½ x ¾ in. Roll the polenta fingers in the flour, then spray or drizzle the remaining olive oil over the fingers.
4. Preheat the air-fryer to 200ºC/400ºF.
5. Lay the fingers apart from one another in a single layer in the preheated air-fryer (you may need to cook these in batches, depending on the size of your air-fryer). Air-fry for 9 minutes, turning once halfway through cooking. Serve immediately with garlic mayonnaise.

Easy Cheesy Scrambled Eggs

Servings: 1
Cooking Time:xx
Ingredients:

- 1 tbsp butter
- 2 eggs
- 100g grated cheese
- 2 tbsp milk
- Salt and pepper for seasoning

Directions:

1. Add the butter inside the air fryer pan and cook at 220ºC until the butter has melted
2. Add the eggs and milk to a bowl and combine, seasoning to your liking
3. Pour the eggs into the butter panned cook for 3 minutes, stirring around lightly to scramble
4. Add the cheese and cook for another 2 more minutes

Monte Cristo Breakfast Sandwich

Servings: 4
Cooking Time:xx
Ingredients:

- 1 egg
- 2 slices of sandwich bread
- 1/4 tsp vanilla extract
- 4 slices of sliced Swiss cheese
- 4 slices of sliced deli ham
- 4 slices of sliced turkey
- 1 tsp melted butter
- Powdered sugar for serving

Directions:

1. In a small bowl, mix together the egg and vanilla extract, combining well
2. Take your bread and assemble your sandwich, starting with a slice of cheese, then the ham, turkey, and then another slice of the cheese, with the other slice of bread on the top
3. Compress the sandwich a little, so it cooks better
4. Take a piece of cooking foil and brush over it with the butter
5. Take your sandwich and dip each side into the egg mixture, leaving it to one side for around half a minute
6. Place the sandwich on the foil and place it inside your fryer
7. Cook at 200ºC for around 10 minutes, before turning the sandwich over and cooking for another 8 minutes
8. Transfer your sandwich onto a plate and sprinkle with a little powdered sugar

Swede Fries

Servings: 4
Cooking Time:xx
Ingredients:

- 1 medium swede/rutabaga
- ½ teaspoon salt
- ½ teaspoon freshly ground black pepper
- 1½ teaspoons dried thyme
- 1 tablespoon olive oil

Directions:

1. Preheat the air-fryer to 160ºC/325ºF.
2. Peel the swede/rutabaga and slice into fries about 6 x 1 cm/2½ x ½ in., then toss the fries in the salt, pepper, thyme and oil, making sure every fry is coated.
3. Tip into the preheated air-fryer in a single layer (you may need to cook them in two batches, depending on the size of your air-fryer) and air-fry for 15 minutes, shaking the drawer halfway through. Then increase the temperature to 180ºC/350ºF and cook for a further 5 minutes. Serve immediately.

Oozing Baked Eggs

Servings: 2
Cooking Time:xx
Ingredients:

- 4 eggs
- 140g smoked gouda cheese, cut into small pieces
- Salt and pepper to taste

Directions:

1. You will need two ramekin dishes and spray each one before using
2. Crack two eggs into each ramekin dish
3. Add half of the Gouda cheese to each dish
4. Season and place into the air fryer
5. Cook at 350ºC for 15 minutes, until the eggs are cooked as you like them

7

Blanket Breakfast Eggs

Servings: 2

Cooking Time:xx

Ingredients:

- 2 eggs
- 2 slices of sandwich bread
- Olive oil spray
- Salt and pepper to taste

Directions:

1. Preheat your air fryer to 190ºC and spray with a little oil
2. Meanwhile, take your bread and cut a hole into the middle of each piece
3. Place one slice inside your fryer and crack one egg into the middle
4. Season with a little salt and pepper
5. Cook for 5 minutes, before turning over and cooking for a further 2 minutes
6. Remove the first slice and repeat the process with the remaining slice of bread and egg

Sweet Potato Fries

Servings: 4

Cooking Time:xx

Ingredients:

- 2 medium sweet potatoes
- 2 teaspoons olive oil
- ½ teaspoon salt
- ½ teaspoon chilli/hot red pepper flakes
- ½ teaspoon smoked paprika

Directions:

1. Preheat the air-fryer to 190ºC/375ºF.
2. Peel the sweet potatoes and slice into fries about 1 x 1 cm/½ x ½ in. by the length of the potato. Toss the sweet potato fries in the oil, salt, chilli and paprika, making sure every fry is coated.
3. Tip into the preheated air-fryer in a single layer (you may need to cook them in two batches, depending on the size of your air-fryer). Air-fry for 10 minutes, turning once halfway during cooking. Serve immediately.

Raspberry Breakfast Pockets

Servings: 1

Cooking Time:xx

Ingredients:

- 2 slices of sandwich bread
- 1 tbsp soft cream cheese
- 1 tbsp raspberry jam
- 1 tbsp milk
- 1 egg

Directions:

1. Take one slice of the bread and add one tablespoon of jam into the middle
2. Take the second slice and add the cream cheese into the middle
3. Using a blunt knife, spread the jam and the cheese across the bread, but don't go to the outer edges
4. Take a small bowl and whisk the eggs and the milk together
5. Set your fryer to 190ºC and spray with a little oil
6. Dip your sandwich into the egg and arrange inside your fryer
7. Cook for 5 minutes on the first side, turn and cook for another 2 minutes

Blueberry & Lemon Breakfast Muffins

Servings: 12
Cooking Time:xx

Ingredients:

- 315g self raising flour
- 65g sugar
- 120ml double cream
- 2 tbsp of light cooking oil
- 2 eggs
- 125g blueberries
- The zest and juice of a lemon
- 1 tsp vanilla

Directions:

1. Take a small bowl and mix the self raising flour and sugar together
2. Take another bowl and mix together the oil, juice, eggs, cream, and vanilla
3. Add this mixture to the flour mixture and blend together
4. Add the blueberries and fold
5. You will need individual muffin holders, silicone works best. Spoon the mixture into the holders
6. Cook at 150ºC for 10 minutes
7. Check at the halfway point to check they're not cooking too fast
8. Remove and allow to cool

Toad In The Hole, Breakfast Style

Servings: 4
Cooking Time:xx

Ingredients:

- 1 sheet of puff pastry (defrosted)
- 4 eggs
- 4 tbsp grated cheese (cheddar works well)
- 4 slices of cooked ham, cut into pieces
- Chopped fresh herbs of your choice

Directions:

1. Preheat your air fryer to 200ºC
2. Take your pastry sheet and place it on a flat surface, cutting it into four pieces
3. Take two of the pastry sheets and place them inside your fryer, cooking for up to 8 minutes, until done
4. Remove the pastry and flatten the centre down with a spoon, to form a deep hole
5. Add a tablespoon of the cheese and a tablespoon of the ham into the hole
6. Crack one egg into the hole
7. Return the pastry to the air fryer and cook for another 6 minutes, or until the egg is done as you like it
8. Remove and allow to cool
9. Repeat the process with the rest of the pastry remaining
10. Sprinkle fresh herbs on top and serve

Morning Sausage Wraps

Servings: 8

Cooking Time:xx

Ingredients:

- 8 sausages, chopped into pieces
- 2 slices of cheddar cheese, cut into quarters
- 1 can of regular crescent roll dough
- 8 wooden skewers

Directions:

1. Take the dough and separate each one
2. Cut open the sausages evenly
3. The one of your crescent rolls and on the widest part, add a little sausage and then a little cheese
4. Roll the dough and tuck it until you form a triangle
5. Repeat this for four times and add into your air fryer
6. Cook at 190ºC for 3 minutes
7. Remove your dough and add a skewer for serving
8. Repeat with the other four pieces of dough

Blueberry Bread

Servings: 8

Cooking Time:xx

Ingredients:

- 260ml milk
- 3 eggs
- 25g protein powder
- 400g frozen blueberries
- 600g bisquick or pancake mixture

Directions:

1. Take a large mixing bowl and combine all ingredients until smooth
2. Preheat the air fryer to 250ºC
3. Place the mixture into a loaf tin
4. Place the tin into the air fryer and cook for 30 minutes
5. A toothpick should come out clean if the bread is cooked

Egg & Bacon Breakfast Cups

Servings: 8

Cooking Time:xx

Ingredients:

- 6 eggs
- 1 chopped red pepper
- 1 chopped green pepper
- 1 chopped yellow pepper
- 2 tbsp double cream
- 50g chopped spinach
- 50g grated cheddar cheese
- 50g grated mozzarella cheese
- 3 slices of cooked bacon, crumbled into pieces

Directions:

1. Take a large mixing bowl and crack the eggs
2. Add the cream and season with a little salt and pepper, combining everything well
3. Add the peppers, spinach, onions, both cheeses, and the crumbled bacon, combining everything once more
4. You will need silicone moulds or cups for this part, and you should pour equal amounts of the mixture into 8 cups
5. Cook at 150ºC for around 12 or 15 minutes, until the eggs are cooked properly

Healthy Stuffed Peppers

Servings: 2
Cooking Time:xx
Ingredients:

- 1 large bell pepper, deseeded and cut into halves
- 1 tsp olive oil
- 4 large eggs
- Salt and pepper to taste

Directions:

1. Take your peppers and rub a little olive oil on the edges
2. Into each pepper, crack one egg and season with salt and pepper
3. You will need to insert a trivet into your air fryer to hold the peppers, and then arrange the peppers evenly
4. Set your fryer to 200°C and cook for 13 minutes
5. Once cooked, remove and serve with a little more seasoning, if required

Cheese Scones

Servings:12
Cooking Time:xx
Ingredients:

- ½ teaspoon baking powder
- 210 g/1½ cups self-raising/self-rising flour (gluten-free if you wish), plus extra for dusting
- 50 g/3½ tablespoons cold butter, cubed
- 125 g/1½ cups grated mature Cheddar
- a pinch of cayenne pepper
- a pinch of salt
- 100 ml/7 tablespoons milk, plus extra for brushing the tops of the scones

Directions:

1. Mix the baking powder with the flour in a bowl, then add the butter and rub into the flour to form a crumblike texture. Add the cheese, cayenne pepper and salt and stir. Then add the milk, a little at a time, and bring together into a ball of dough.
2. Dust your work surface with flour. Roll the dough flat until about 1.5 cm/⅝ in. thick. Cut out the scones using a 6-cm/2½-in. diameter cookie cutter. Gather the offcuts into a ball, re-roll and cut more scones – you should get about 12 scones from the mixture. Place the scones on an air-fryer liner or a piece of pierced parchment paper.
3. Preheat the air-fryer to 180°C/350°F.
4. Add the scones to the preheated air-fryer and air-fry for 8 minutes, turning them over halfway to cook the other side. Remove and allow to cool a little, then serve warm.

Apple Crisps

Servings: 2
Cooking Time:xx
Ingredients:

- 2 apples, chopped
- 1 tsp cinnamon
- 2 tbsp brown sugar
- 1 tsp lemon juice
- 2.5 tbsp plain flour
- 3 tbsp oats
- 2 tbsp cold butter
- Pinch of salt

Directions:

1. Preheat the air fryer to 260°C
2. Take a 5" baking dish and crease
3. Take a large bowl and combine the apples with the sugar, cinnamon and lemon juice
4. Add the mixture to the baking dish and cover with aluminium foil
5. Place in the air fryer and cook for 15 minutes
6. Open the lid and cook for another 5 minutes
7. Combine the rest of the ingredients in a food processor, until a crumble-type mixture occurs
8. Add over the top of the cooked apples
9. Cook with the lid open for another 5 minutes
10. Allow to cool a little before serving

Cumin Shoestring Carrots

Servings: 2

Cooking Time:xx

Ingredients:

- 300 g/10½ oz. carrots
- 1 teaspoon cornflour/cornstarch
- 1 teaspoon ground cumin
- ¼ teaspoon salt
- 1 tablespoon olive oil
- garlic mayonnaise, to serve

Directions:

1. Preheat the air-fryer to 200ºC/400ºF.

2. Peel the carrots and cut into thin fries, roughly 10 cm x 1 cm x 5 mm/4 x ½ x ¼ in. Toss the carrots in a bowl with all the other ingredients.

3. Add the carrots to the preheated air-fryer and air-fry for 9 minutes, shaking the drawer of the air-fryer a couple of times during cooking. Serve with garlic mayo on the side.

Plantain Fries

Servings: 2

Cooking Time:xx

Ingredients:

- 1 ripe plantain (yellow and brown outside skin)
- 1 teaspoon olive oil
- ¼ teaspoon salt

Directions:

1. Preheat the air-fryer to 180ºC/350ºF.

2. Peel the plantain and slice into fries about 6 x 1 cm/2½ x ½ in. Toss the fries in oil and salt, making sure every fry is coated.

3. Tip into the preheated air-fryer in a single layer (you may need to cook them in two batches, depending on the size of your air-fryer) and air-fry for 13–14 minutes until brown on the outside and soft on the inside. Serve immediately.

French Toast

Servings: 2

Cooking Time:xx

Ingredients:

- 2 beaten eggs
- 2 tbsp softened butter
- 4 slices of sandwich bread
- 1 tsp cinnamon
- 1 tsp nutmeg
- 1 tsp ground cloves
- 1 tsp maple syrup

Directions:

1. Preheat your fryer to 180ºC

2. Take a bowl and add the eggs, salt, cinnamon, nutmeg, and cloves, combining well

3. Take your bread and butter each side, cutting into strips

4. Dip the bread slices into the egg mixture

5. Arrange each slice into the basket of your fryer

6. Cook for 2 minutes

7. Take the basket out and spray with a little cooking spray

8. Turn over the slices and place back into the fryer

9. Cook for 4 minutes

10. Remove and serve with maple syrup

Halloumi Fries

Servings: 2
Cooking Time:xx
Ingredients:

- 225 g/8 oz. halloumi
- 40 g/heaped ¼ cup plain/all-purpose flour (gluten-free if you wish)
- ½ teaspoon sweet smoked paprika
- ½ teaspoon dried oregano
- ¼ teaspoon mild chilli/chili powder
- olive oil or avocado oil, for spraying

Directions:

1. Preheat the air-fryer to 180°C/350°F.
2. Slice the halloumi into fries roughly 2 x 1.5 cm/¾ x ⅝ in.
3. Mix the flour and seasoning in a bowl and dip each halloumi stick into the flour to coat. Spray with a little oil.
4. Add the fries to the preheated air-fryer and air-fry for 5 minutes. Serve immediately.

Bocconcini Balls

Servings: 2
Cooking Time:xx
Ingredients:

- 70 g/½ cup plus ½ tablespoon plain/all-purpose flour (gluten-free if you wish)
- 1 egg, beaten
- 70 g/1 cup dried breadcrumbs (gluten-free if you wish; see page 9)
- 10 bocconcini

Directions:

1. Preheat the air-fryer to 200°C/400°F.
2. Place the flour, egg and breadcrumbs on 3 separate plates. Dip each bocconcini ball first in the flour to coat, then the egg, shaking off any excess before rolling in the breadcrumbs.
3. Add the breaded bocconcini to the preheated air-fryer and air-fry for 5 minutes (no need to turn them during cooking). Serve immediately.

Tangy Breakfast Hash

Servings: 6
Cooking Time:xx
Ingredients:

- 2 tbsp olive oil
- 2 sweet potatoes, cut into cubes
- 1 tbsp smoked paprika
- 1 tsp salt
- 1 tsp black pepper
- 2 slices of bacon, cut into small pieces

Directions:

1. Preheat your air fryer to 200°C
2. Pour the olive oil into a large mixing bowl
3. Add the bacon, seasonings, potatoes and toss to evenly coat
4. Transfer the mixture into the air fryer and cook for 12-16 minutes
5. Stir after 10 minutes and continue to stir periodically for another 5 minutes

Sauces & Snack And Appetiser Recipes

Cheesy Taco Crescents

Servings: 8
Cooking Time:xx
Ingredients:

- 1 can Pillsbury crescent sheets, or alternative
- 4 Monterey Jack cheese sticks
- 150g browned minced beef
- ½ pack taco seasoning mix

Directions:

1. Preheat the air fryer to 200ºC
2. Combine the minced beef and the taco seasoning, warm in the microwave for about 2 minutes
3. Cut the crescent sheets into 8 equal squares
4. Cut the cheese sticks in half
5. Add half a cheese stick to each square, and 2 tablespoons of mince
6. Roll up the dough and pinch at the ends to seal
7. Place in the air fryer and cook for 5 minutes
8. Turnover and cook for another 3 minutes

Pepperoni Bread

Servings: 4
Cooking Time:xx
Ingredients:

- Cooking spray
- 400g pizza dough
- 200g pepperoni
- 1 tbsp dried oregano
- Ground pepper to taste
- Garlic salt to taste
- 1 tsp melted butter
- 1 tsp grated parmesan
- 50g grated mozzarella

Directions:

1. Line a baking tin with 2 inch sides with foil to fit in the air fryer
2. Spray with cooking spray
3. Preheat the air fryer to 200ºC
4. Roll the pizza dough into 1 inch balls and line the baking tin
5. Sprinkle with pepperoni, oregano, pepper and garlic salt
6. Brush with melted butter and sprinkle with parmesan
7. Place in the air fryer and cook for 15 minutes
8. Sprinkle with mozzarella and cook for another 2 minutes

Corn Nuts

Servings: 8
Cooking Time:xx

Ingredients:

- 1 giant white corn
- 3 tbsp vegetable oil
- 2 tsp salt

Directions:

1. Place the corn in a large bowl, cover with water and sit for 8 hours
2. Drain, pat dry and air dry for 20 minutes
3. Preheat the air fryer to 200ºC
4. Place in a bowl and coat with oil and salt
5. Cook in the air fryer for 10 minutes shake then cook for a further 10 minutes

Pasta Chips

Servings: 2
Cooking Time:xx

Ingredients:

- 300g dry pasta bows
- 1 tbsp olive oil
- 1 tbsp nutritional yeast
- 1½ tsp Italian seasoning
- ½ tsp salt

Directions:

1. Cook the pasta for half the time stated on the packet
2. Drain and mix with the oil, yeast, seasoning and salt
3. Place in the air fryer and cook at 200ºC for 5 minutes shake and cook for a further 3 minutes until crunchy

Bacon Smokies

Servings: 8
Cooking Time:xx

Ingredients:

- 150g little smokies (pieces)
- 150g bacon
- 50g brown sugar
- Toothpicks

Directions:

1. Cut the bacon strips into thirds
2. Put the brown sugar into a bowl
3. Coat the bacon with the sugar
4. Wrap the bacon around the little smokies and secure with a toothpick
5. Heat the air fryer to 170ºC
6. Place in the air fryer and cook for 10 minutes until crispy

Salt And Vinegar Chickpeas

Servings: 5
Cooking Time:xx

Ingredients:

- 1 can chickpeas
- 100ml white vinegar
- 1 tbsp olive oil
- Salt to taste

Directions:

1. Combine chickpeas and vinegar in a pan, simmer remove from heat and stand for 30 minutes
2. Preheat the air fryer to 190ºC
3. Drain chickpeas
4. Place chickpeas in the air fryer and cook for about 4 minutes
5. Pour chickpeas into an ovenproof bowl drizzle with oil, sprinkle with salt
6. Place bowl in the air fryer and cook for another 4 minutes

Cheese Wontons

Servings: 8
Cooking Time:xx

Ingredients:

- 8 wonton wrappers
- 1 carton pimento cheese
- Small dish of water
- Cooking spray

Directions:

1. Place one tsp of cheese in the middle of each wonton wrapper
2. Brush the edges of each wonton wrapper with water
3. Fold over to create a triangle and seal
4. Heat the air fryer to 190ºC
5. Spray the wontons with cooking spray
6. Place in the air fryer and cook for 3 minutes
7. Turnover and cook for a further 3 minutes

Pao De Queijo

Servings: 20
Cooking Time:xx

Ingredients:

- 150g sweet starch
- 150g sour starch
- 50ml milk
- 25ml water
- 25ml olive oil
- 1 tsp salt
- 2 eggs
- 100g grated cheese
- 50g grated parmesan

Directions:

1. Preheat the air fryer to 170ºC
2. Mix the starch together in a bowl until well mixed
3. Add olive oil, milk and water to a pan, bring to the boil and reduce the heat
4. Add the starch and mix until all the liquid is absorbed
5. Add the eggs and mix to a dough
6. Add the cheeses and mix well
7. Form the dough into balls
8. Line the air fryer with parchment paper
9. Bake in the air fryer for 8-10 minutes

Spring Rolls

Servings: 20
Cooking Time:xx
Ingredients:

- 160g dried rice noodles
- 1 tsp sesame oil
- 300g minced beef
- 200g frozen vegetables
- 1 onion, diced
- 3 cloves garlic, crushed
- 1 tsp soy sauce
- 1 tbsp vegetable oil
- 1 pack egg roll wrappers

Directions:

1. Soak the noodles in a bowl of water until soft
2. Add the minced beef, onion, garlic and vegetables to a pan and cook for 6 minutes
3. Remove from the heat, stir in the noodles and add the soy
4. Heat the air fryer to 175°C
5. Add a diagonal strip of filling in each egg roll wrapper
6. Fold the top corner over the filling, fold in the two side corners
7. Brush the centre with water and roll to seal
8. Brush with vegetable oil, place in the air fryer and cook for about 8 minutes until browned

Mozzarella Sticks

Servings: 4
Cooking Time:xx
Ingredients:

- 60ml water
- 50g flour
- 5 tbsp cornstarch
- 1 tbsp cornmeal
- 1 tsp garlic powder
- ½ tsp salt
- 100g breadcrumbs
- ½ tsp pepper
- ½ tsp parsley
- ½ tsp onion powder
- ¼ tsp oregano
- ½ tsp basil
- 200g mozzarella cut into ½ inch strips

Directions:

1. Mix water, flour, cornstarch, cornmeal, garlic powder and salt in a bowl
2. Stir breadcrumbs, pepper, parsley, onion powder, oregano and basil together in another bowl
3. Dip the mozzarella sticks in the batter then coat in the breadcrumbs
4. Heat the air fryer to 200°C
5. Cook for 6 minutes turn and cook for another 6 minutes

Mac & Cheese Bites

Servings: 14
Cooking Time:xx

Ingredients:

- 200g mac and cheese
- 2 eggs
- 200g panko breadcrumbs
- Cooking spray

Directions:

1. Place drops of mac and cheese on parchment paper and freeze for 1 hour
2. Beat the eggs in a bowl, add the breadcrumbs to another bowl
3. Dip the mac and cheese balls in the egg then into the breadcrumbs
4. Heat the air fryer to 190ºC
5. Place in the air fryer, spray with cooking spray and cook for 15 minutes

Tortellini Bites

Servings: 6
Cooking Time:xx

Ingredients:

- 200g cheese tortellini
- 150g flour
- 100g panko bread crumbs
- 50g grated parmesan
- 1 tsp dried oregano
- 2 eggs
- ½ tsp garlic powder
- ½ tsp chilli flakes
- Salt
- Pepper

Directions:

1. Cook the tortellini according to the packet instructions
2. Mix the panko, parmesan, oregano, garlic powder, chilli flakes salt and pepper in a bowl
3. Beat the eggs in another bowl and place the flour in a third bowl
4. Coat the tortellini in flour, then egg and then in the panko mix
5. Place in the air fryer and cook at 185ºC for 10 minutes until crispy
6. Serve with marinara sauce for dipping

Spicy Chickpeas

Servings: 4
Cooking Time:xx

Ingredients:

- 1 can chickpeas
- 1 tbsp yeast
- 1 tbsp olive oil
- 1 tsp paprika
- 1 tsp garlic powder
- ½ tsp salt
- Pinch cumin

Directions:

1. Preheat air fryer to 180ºC
2. Combine all ingredients
3. Add to the air fryer and cook for 22 minutes tossing every 4 minutes until cooked

Pork Jerky

Servings: 35
Cooking Time:xx
Ingredients:

- 300g mince pork
- 1 tbsp oil
- 1 tbsp sriracha
- 1 tbsp soy
- ½ tsp pink curing salt
- 1 tbsp rice vinegar
- ½ tsp salt
- ½ tsp pepper
- ½ tsp onion powder

Directions:

1. Mix all ingredients in a bowl until combined
2. Refrigerate for about 8 hours
3. Shape into sticks and place in the air fryer
4. Heat the air fryer to 160ºC
5. Cook for 1 hour turn then cook for another hour
6. Turn again and cook for another hour
7. Cover with paper and sit for 8 hours

Jalapeño Pockets

Servings: 4
Cooking Time:xx
Ingredients:

- 1 chopped onion
- 60g cream cheese
- 1 jalapeño, chopped
- 8 wonton wrappers
- ¼ tsp garlic powder
- ⅛ tsp onion powder

Directions:

1. Cook the onion in a pan for 5 minutes until softened
2. Add to a bowl and mix with the remaining ingredients
3. Lay the wonton wrappers out and add filling to each one
4. Fold over to create a triangle and seal with water around the edges
5. Heat the air fryer to 200ºC
6. Place in the air fryer and cook for about 4 minutes

Onion Pakoda

Servings: 2
Cooking Time:xx
Ingredients:

- 200g gram flour
- 2 onions, thinly sliced
- 1 tbsp crushed coriander seeds
- 1 tsp chilli powder
- ¾ tsp salt
- ¼ tsp turmeric
- ¼ tsp baking soda

Directions:

1. Mix all the ingredients together in a large bowl
2. Make bite sized pakodas
3. Heat the air fryer to 200ºC
4. Line the air fryer with foil
5. Place the pakoda in the air fryer and cook for 5 minutes
6. Turn over and cook for a further 5 minutes

Italian Rice Balls

Servings: 2

Cooking Time:xx

Ingredients:

- 400g cooked rice
- 25g breadcrumbs, plus an extra 200g for breading
- 2 tbsp flour, plus an extra 2 tbsp for breading
- 1 tbsp cornstarch, plus an extra 3 tbsp for breading
- 1 chopped bell pepper
- 1 chopped onion
- 2 tbsp olive oil
- 1 tsp red chilli flakes
- 5 chopped mozzarella cheese sticks
- A little water for the breading
- Salt and pepper for seasoning

Directions:

1. Place the cooked rice into a bowl and mash with a fork. Place to one side
2. Take a saucepan and add the oil, salting the onion and peppers until they're both soft
3. Add the chilli flakes and a little salt and combine
4. Add the mixture to the mashed rice and combine
5. Add the 2 tbsp flour and 1 tbsp cornstarch, along with the 25g breadcrumbs and combine well
6. Use your hands to create balls with the mixture
7. Stuff a piece of the mozzarella inside the balls and form around it
8. Take a bowl and add the rest of the flour, corn starch and a little seasoning, with a small amount of water to create a thick batter
9. Take another bowl and add the rest of the breadcrumbs
10. Dip each rice ball into the batter and then the breadcrumbs
11. Preheat the air fryer to 220ºC
12. Cook for 6 minutes, before shaking and cooking for another 6 minutes

Pretzel Bites

Servings: 2

Cooking Time:xx

Ingredients:

- 650g flour
- 2.5 tsp active dry yeast
- 260ml hot water
- 1 tsp salt
- 4 tbsp melted butter
- 2 tbsp sugar

Directions:

1. Take a large bowl and add the flour, sugar and salt
2. Take another bowl and combine the hot water and yeast, stirring until the yeast has dissolved
3. Then, add the yeast mixture to the flour mixture and use your hands to combine
4. Knead for 2 minutes
5. Cover the bowl with a kitchen towel for around half an hour
6. Divide the dough into 6 pieces
7. Preheat the air fryer to 260ºC
8. Take each section of dough and tear off a piece, rolling it in your hands to create a rope shape, that is around 1" in thickness
9. Cut into 2" strips
10. Place the small dough balls into the air fryer and leave a little space in-between
11. Cook for 6 minutes
12. Once cooked, remove and brush with melted butter and sprinkle salt on top

Beetroot Crisps

Servings: 2
Cooking Time:xx
Ingredients:

- 3 medium beetroots
- 2 tbsp oil
- Salt to taste

Directions:

1. Peel and thinly slice the beetroot
2. Coat with the oil and season with salt
3. Preheat the air fryer to 200°C
4. Place in the air fryer and cook for 12-18 minutes until crispy

Snack Style Falafel

Servings: 15
Cooking Time:xx
Ingredients:

- 150g dry garbanzo beans
- 300g coriander
- 75g flat leaf parsley
- 1 red onion, quartered
- 1 clove garlic
- 2 tbsp chickpea flour
- Cooking spray
- 1 tbsp cumin
- 1 tbsp coriander
- 1 tbsp sriracha
- ½ tsp baking powder
- Salt and pepper to taste
- ¼ tsp baking soda

Directions:

1. Add all ingredients apart from the baking soda and baking powder to a food processor and blend well
2. Cover and rest for 1 hour
3. Heat air fryer to 190°C
4. Add baking powder and baking soda to mix and combine
5. Form mix into 15 equal balls
6. Spray air fryer with cooking spray
7. Add to air fryer and cook for 8-10 minutes

Roasted Almonds

Servings: 2
Cooking Time:xx

Ingredients:

- 1 tbsp soy sauce
- 1 tbsp garlic powder
- 1 tsp paprika
- ¼ tsp pepper
- 400g raw almonds

Directions:

1. Place all of the ingredients apart from the almonds in a bowl and mix
2. Add the almonds and coat well
3. Place the almonds in the air fryer and cook at 160°C for 6 minutes shaking every 2 minutes

Jalapeño Poppers

Servings: 2
Cooking Time:xx

Ingredients:

- 10 jalapeños, halved and deseeded
- 100g cream cheese
- 50g parsley
- 150g breadcrumbs

Directions:

1. Mix 1/2 the breadcrumbs with the cream cheese
2. Add the parsley
3. Stuff the peppers with the cream cheese mix
4. Top the peppers with the remaining breadcrumbs
5. Heat the air fryer to 185°C
6. Place in the air fryer and cook for 6-8 minutes

Poultry Recipes

Air Fryer Sesame Chicken Thighs

Servings: 4

Cooking Time:xx

Ingredients:

- 2 tbsp sesame oil
- 2 tbsp soy sauce
- 1 tbsp honey
- 1 tbsp sriracha sauce
- 1 tsp rice vinegar
- 400g chicken thighs
- 1 green onion, chopped
- 2 tbsp toasted sesame seeds

Directions:

1. Take a large bowl and combine the sesame oil, soy sauce, honey, sriracha and vinegar
2. Add the chicken and refrigerate for 30 minutes
3. Preheat the air fryer to 200°C
4. Cook for 5 minutes
5. Flip and then cook for another 10 minutes
6. Serve with green onion and sesame seeds

Chicken Balls, Greek-style

Servings: 4

Cooking Time:xx

Ingredients:

- 500g ground chicken
- 1 egg
- 1 tbsp dried oregano
- 1.5 tbsp garlic paste
- 1 tsp lemon zest
- 1 tsp dried onion powder
- Salt and pepper to taste

Directions:

1. Take a bowl and combine all ingredients well
2. Use your hands to create meatballs - you should be able to make 12 balls
3. Preheat your air fryer to 260°C
4. Add the meatballs to the fryer and cook for 9 minutes

Chicken Tikka

Servings: 2
Cooking Time:xx
Ingredients:

- 2 chicken breasts, diced
- FIRST MARINADE
- freshly squeezed juice of ½ a lemon
- 1 tablespoon freshly grated ginger
- 1 tablespoon freshly grated garlic
- a good pinch of salt
- SECOND MARINADE
- 100 g/½ cup Greek yogurt
- ½ teaspoon chilli powder
- ½ teaspoon chilli paste
- ½ teaspoon turmeric
- ½ teaspoon garam masala
- 1 tablespoon olive oil

Directions:

1. Mix the ingredients for the first marinade together in a bowl, add in the chicken and stir to coat all the chicken pieces. Leave in the fridge to marinate for 20 minutes.

2. Combine the second marinade ingredients. Once the first marinade has had 20 minutes, add the second marinade to the chicken and stir well. Leave in the fridge for at least 4 hours.

3. Preheat the air-fryer to 180ºC/350ºF.

4. Thread the chicken pieces onto metal skewers that fit in your air-fryer. Add the skewers to the preheated air-fryer and air-fry for 10 minutes. Check the internal temperature of the chicken has reached at least 74ºC/165ºF using a meat thermometer – if not, cook for another few minutes and then serve.

Sticky Chicken Tikka Drumsticks

Servings: 4
Cooking Time:xx
Ingredients:

- 12 chicken drumsticks
- MARINADE
- 100 g/½ cup Greek yogurt
- 2 tablespoons tikka paste
- 2 teaspoons ginger preserve
- freshly squeezed juice of ½ a lemon
- ¾ teaspoon salt

Directions:

1. Make slices across each of the drumsticks with a sharp knife. Mix the marinade ingredients together in a bowl, then add the drumsticks. Massage the marinade into the drumsticks, then leave to marinate in the fridge overnight or for at least 6 hours.

2. Preheat the air-fryer to 200ºC/400ºF.

3. Lay the drumsticks on an air-fryer liner or a piece of pierced parchment paper. Place the paper and drumsticks in the preheated air-fryer. Air-fry for 6 minutes, then turn over and cook for a further 6 minutes. Check the internal temperature of the drumsticks has reached at least 75ºC/167ºF using a meat thermometer – if not, cook for another few minutes and then serve.

Buffalo Chicken Wontons

Servings: 6

Cooking Time:xx

Ingredients:

- 200g shredded chicken
- 1 tbsp buffalo sauce
- 4 tbsp softened cream cheese
- 1 sliced spring onion
- 2 tbsp blue cheese crumbles
- 12 wonton wrappers

Directions:

1. Preheat the air fryer to 200ºC
2. Take a bowl and combine the chicken and buffalo sauce
3. In another bowl mix the cream cheese until a smooth consistency has formed and then combine the scallion blue cheese and seasoned chicken
4. Take the wonton wrappers and run wet fingers along each edge
5. Place 1 tbsp of the filling into the centre of the wonton and fold the corners together
6. Cook at 200ºC for 3 to 5 minutes, until golden brown

Spicy Chicken Wing Drummettes

Servings: 4

Cooking Time:xx

Ingredients:

- 10 large chicken drumettes
- Cooking spray
- 100ml rice vinegar
- 3 tbsp honey
- 2 tbsp unsalted chicken stock
- 1 tbsp lower sodium soy sauce
- 1 tbsp toasted sesame oil
- ⅜ tsp crushed red pepper
- 1 garlic clove, finely chopped
- 2 tbsp chopped, unsalted, roasted peanuts
- 1 tbsp chopped fresh chives

Directions:

1. Coat the chicken in cooking spray and place inside the air fryer
2. Cook at 200ºC for 30 minutes
3. Take a mixing bowl and combine the vinegar, honey, stock, soy sauce, oil, crushed red pepper and garlic
4. Cook to a simmer, until a syrup consistency is achieved
5. Coat the chicken in this mixture and sprinkle with peanuts and chives

Turkey And Mushroom Burgers

Servings: 2

Cooking Time:xx

Ingredients:

- 180g mushrooms
- 500g minced turkey
- 1 tbsp of your favourite chicken seasoning, e.g. Maggi
- 1 tsp onion powder
- 1 tsp garlic powder
- Salt and pepper to taste

Directions:

1. Place the mushrooms in a food processor and puree
2. Add all the seasonings and mix well
3. Remove from the food processor and transfer to a mixing bowl
4. Add the minced turkey and combine again
5. Shape the mix into 5 burger patties
6. Spray with cooking spray and place in the air fryer
7. Cook at 160°C for 10 minutes, until cooked.

Air Fryer Chicken Thigh Schnitzel

Servings: 4

Cooking Time:xx

Ingredients:

- 300g boneless chicken thighs
- 160g seasoned breadcrumbs
- 1 tsp salt
- ½ tsp ground black pepper
- 30g flour
- 1 egg
- Cooking spray

Directions:

1. Lay the chicken on a sheet of parchment paper and add another on top
2. Use a mallet or a rolling pin to flatten it down
3. Take a bowl and add the breadcrumbs with the salt and pepper
4. Place the flour into another bowl
5. Dip the chicken into the flour, then the egg, and then the breadcrumbs
6. Preheat air fryer to 190°C
7. Place the chicken into the air fryer and spray with cooking oil
8. Cook for 6 minutes

Chicken Kiev

Servings: 4
Cooking Time:xx

Ingredients:

- 4 boneless chicken breasts
- 4 tablespoons plain/all-purpose flour (gluten-free if you wish)
- 1 egg, beaten
- 130 g/2 cups dried breadcrumbs (gluten-free if you wish, see page 9)
- GARLIC BUTTER
- 60 g/4 tablespoons salted butter, softened
- 1 large garlic clove, finely chopped

Directions:

1. Mash together the butter and garlic. Form into a sausage shape, then slice into 4 equal discs. Place in the freezer until frozen.
2. Make a deep horizontal slit across each chicken breast, taking care not to cut through to the other side. Stuff the cavity with a disc of frozen garlic butter. Place the flour in a shallow bowl, the egg in another and the breadcrumbs in a third. Coat each chicken breast first in flour, then egg, then breadcrumbs.
3. Preheat the air-fryer to 180ºC/350ºF.
4. Add the chicken Kievs to the preheated air-fryer and air-fry for 12 minutes until cooked through. This is hard to gauge as the butter inside the breast is not an indicator of doneness, so test the meat in the centre with a meat thermometer – it should be at least 75ºC/167ºF; if not, cook for another few minutes.

Crunchy Chicken Tenders

Servings: 4
Cooking Time:xx

Ingredients:

- 8 regular chicken tenders (frozen work best)
- 1 egg
- 2 tbsp olive oil
- 150g dried breadcrumbs

Directions:

1. Heat the fryer to 175ºC
2. In a small bowl, beat the egg
3. In another bowl, combine the oil and the breadcrumbs together
4. Take one tender and first dip it into the egg, and then cover it in the breadcrumb mixture
5. Place the tender into the fryer basket
6. Repeat with the rest of the tenders, arranging them carefully so they don't touch inside the basket
7. Cook for 12 minutes, checking that they are white in the centre before serving

Chicken & Potatoes

Servings: 4

Cooking Time:xx

Ingredients:

- 2 tbsp olive oil
- 2 potatoes, cut into 2" pieces
- 2 chicken breasts, cut into pieces of around 1" size
- 4 crushed garlic cloves
- 2 tsp smoked paprika
- 1 tsp thyme
- 1/2 tsp red chilli flakes
- Salt and pepper to taste

Directions:

1. Preheat your air fryer to 260ºC
2. Take a large bowl and combine the potatoes with half of the garlic, half the paprika, half the chilli flakes, salt, pepper and half the oil
3. Place into the air fryer and cook for 5 minutes, before turning over and cooking for another 5 minutes
4. Take a bowl and add the chicken with the rest of the seasonings and oil, until totally coated
5. Add the chicken to the potatoes mixture, moving the potatoes to the side
6. Cook for 10 minutes, turning the chicken halfway through

Buttermilk Chicken

Servings: 4

Cooking Time:xx

Ingredients:

- 500g chicken thighs, skinless and boneless
- 180ml buttermilk
- 40g tapioca flour
- ½ tsp garlic salt
- 1 egg
- 75g all purpose flour
- ½ tsp brown sugar
- 1 tsp garlic powder
- ½ tsp paprika
- ½ tsp onion powder
- ¼ tsp oregano
- Salt and pepper to taste

Directions:

1. Take a medium mixing bowl and combine the buttermilk and hot sauce
2. Add the tapioca flour, garlic salt and black pepper in a plastic bag and shake
3. Beat the egg
4. Take the chicken thighs and tip into the buttermilk, then the tapioca mixture, the egg, and then the flour
5. Preheat air fryer to 190ºC
6. Cook the chicken thighs for 10 minutes, until white in the middle

Air Fried Maple Chicken Thighs

Servings: 4
Cooking Time:xx
Ingredients:
- 200ml buttermilk
- ½ tbsp maple syrup
- 1 egg
- 1 tsp granulated garlic salt
- 4 chicken thighs with the bone in
- 140g all purpose flour
- 65g tapioca flour
- 1 tsp sweet paprika
- 1 tsp onion powder
- ¼ tsp ground black pepper
- ¼ tsp cayenne pepper
- ½ tsp granulated garlic
- ½ tsp honey powder

Directions:
1. Take a bowl and combine the buttermilk, maple syrup, egg and garlic powder
2. Transfer to a bag and add chicken thighs, shaking to combine well
3. Set aside for 1 hour
4. Take a shallow bowl and add the flour, tapioca flour, salt, sweet paprika, smoked paprika, pepper, cayenne pepper and honey powder, combining well
5. Preheat the air fryer to 190ºC
6. Drag the chicken through flour mixture and place the chicken skin side down in the air fryer Cook for 12 minutes, until white in the middle

Olive Stained Turkey Breast

Servings: 14
Cooking Time:xx
Ingredients:
- The brine from a can of olives
- 150ml buttermilk
- 300g boneless and skinless turkey breasts
- 1 sprig fresh rosemary
- 2 sprigs fresh thyme

Directions:
1. Take a mixing bowl and combine the olive brine and buttermilk
2. Pour the mixture over the turkey breast
3. Add the rosemary and thyme sprigs
4. Place into the refrigerator for 8 hours
5. Remove from the fridge and let the turkey reach room temperature
6. Preheat the air fryer to 175C
7. Cook for 15 minutes, ensuring the turkey is cooked through before serving

Nashville Chicken

Servings: 4

Cooking Time:xx

Ingredients:

- 400g boneless chicken breast tenders
- 2 tsp salt
- 2 tsp coarsely ground black pepper
- 2 tbsp hot sauce
- 2 tbsp pickle juice
- 500g all purpose flour
- 3 large eggs
- 300ml buttermilk
- 2 tbsp olive oil
- 6 tbsp cayenne pepper
- 3 tbsp dark brown sugar
- 1 tsp chilli powder
- 1 tsp garlic powder
- 1 tsp paprika
- Salt and pepper to taste

Directions:

1. Take a large mixing bowl and add the chicken, hot sauce, pickle juice, salt and pepper and combine
2. Place in the refrigerator for 3 hours
3. Transfer the flour to a bowl
4. Take another bowl and add the eggs, buttermilk and 1 tbsp of the hot sauce, combining well
5. Press each piece of chicken into the flour and coat well
6. Place the chicken into the buttermilk mixture and then back into the flour
7. Allow to sit or 10 minutes
8. Preheat the air fryer to 193C
9. Whisk together the spices, brown sugar and olive oil to make the sauce and pour over the chicken tenders
10. Serve whilst still warm

Pepper & Lemon Chicken Wings

Servings: 2

Cooking Time:xx

Ingredients:

- 1kg chicken wings
- 1/4 tsp cayenne pepper
- 2 tsp lemon pepper seasoning
- 3 tbsp butter
- 1 tsp honey
- An extra 1 tsp lemon pepper seasoning for the sauce

Directions:

1. Preheat the air fryer to 260°C
2. Place the lemon pepper seasoning and cayenne in a bowl and combine
3. Coat the chicken in the seasoning
4. Place the chicken in the air fryer and cook for 20 minutes, turning over halfway
5. Turn the temperature up to 300°C and cook for another 6 minutes
6. Meanwhile, melt the butter and combine with the honey and the rest of the seasoning
7. Remove the wings from the air fryer and pour the sauce over the top

Grain-free Chicken Katsu

Servings: 4
Cooking Time:xx

Ingredients:

- 125 g/1¼ cups ground almonds
- ½ teaspoon salt
- ½ teaspoon garlic powder
- ½ teaspoon dried parsley
- ½ teaspoon freshly ground black pepper
- ¼ teaspoon onion powder
- ¼ teaspoon dried oregano
- 450 g/1 lb. mini chicken fillets
- 1 egg, beaten
- oil, for spraying/drizzling
- coriander/cilantro leaves, to serve
- KATSU SAUCE
- 1 teaspoon olive oil or avocado oil
- 1 courgette/zucchini (approx. 150 g/5 oz.), finely chopped
- 1 carrot (approx. 100 g/3½ oz.), finely chopped
- 1 onion (approx. 120 g/4½ oz.), finely chopped
- 1 eating apple (approx. 150 g/5 oz.), cored and finely chopped
- 1 teaspoon ground ginger
- 1 teaspoon ground turmeric
- 2 teaspoons ground cumin
- 2 teaspoons ground coriander
- 1½ teaspoons mild chilli/chili powder
- 1 teaspoon garlic powder
- 1½ tablespoons runny honey
- 1 tablespoon soy sauce (gluten-free if you wish)
- 700 ml/3 cups vegetable stock (700 ml/3 cups water with 1½ stock cubes)

Directions:

1. First make the sauce. The easiest way to ensure all the vegetables and apple are finely chopped is to combine them in a food processor. Heat the oil in a large saucepan and sauté the finely chopped vegetables and apple for 5 minutes. Add all the seasonings, honey, soy sauce and stock and stir well, then bring to a simmer and simmer for 30 minutes.
2. Meanwhile, mix together the ground almonds, seasonings and spices. Dip each chicken fillet into the beaten egg, then into the almond-spice mix, making sure each fillet is fully coated. Spray the coated chicken fillets with olive oil (or simply drizzle over).
3. Preheat the air-fryer to 180°C/350°F.
4. Place the chicken fillets in the preheated air-fryer and air-fry for 10 minutes, turning halfway through cooking. Check the internal temperature of the chicken has reached at least 74°C/165°F using a meat thermometer – if not, cook for another few minutes.
5. Blend the cooked sauce in a food processor until smooth. Serve the chicken with the Katsu Sauce drizzled over (if necessary, reheat the sauce gently before serving) and scattered with coriander leaves. Any unused sauce can be frozen.

Turkey Cutlets In Mushroom Sauce

Servings: 2
Cooking Time:xx

Ingredients:

- 2 turkey cutlets
- 1 tbsp butter
- 1 can of cream of mushroom sauce
- 160ml milk
- Salt and pepper for seasoning

Directions:

1. Preheat the air fryer to 220°C
2. Brush the turkey cults with the butter and seasoning
3. Place in the air fryer and cook for 11 minutes
4. Add the mushroom soup and milk to a pan and cook over the stone for around 10 minutes, stirring every so often
5. Top the turkey cutlets with the sauce

Pizza Chicken Nuggets

Servings: 2
Cooking Time:xx
Ingredients:

- 60 g/¾ cup dried breadcrumbs (see page 9)
- 20 g/¼ cup grated Parmesan
- ½ teaspoon dried oregano
- ¼ teaspoon freshly ground black pepper
- 150 g/⅔ cup Mediterranean sauce (see page 102) or 150 g/5½ oz. jarred tomato pasta sauce (keep any leftover sauce for serving)
- 400 g/14 oz. chicken fillets

Directions:

1. Preheat the air-fryer to 180ºC/350ºF.
2. Combine the breadcrumbs, Parmesan, oregano and pepper in a bowl. Have the Mediterranean or pasta sauce in a separate bowl
3. Dip each chicken fillet in the tomato sauce first, then roll in the breadcrumb mix until coated fully.
4. Add the breaded fillets to the preheated air-fryer and air-fry for 10 minutes. Check the internal temperature of the chicken has reached at least 74ºC/165ºF using a meat thermometer – if not, cook for another few minutes.
5. Serve with some additional sauce that has been warmed through.

Chicken And Cheese Chimichangas

Servings: 6
Cooking Time:xx
Ingredients:

- 100g shredded chicken (cooked)
- 150g nacho cheese
- 1 chopped jalapeño pepper
- 6 flour tortillas
- 5 tbsp salsa
- 60g refried beans
- 1 tsp cumin
- 0.5 tsp chill powder
- Salt and pepper to taste

Directions:

1. Take a large mixing bowl and add all of the ingredients, combining well
2. Add ⅓ of the filling to each tortilla and roll into a burrito shape
3. Spray the air fryer with cooking spray and heat to 200ºC
4. Place the chimichangas in the air fryer and cook for 7 minutes

Crispy Cornish Hen

Servings: 4
Cooking Time:xx
Ingredients:

- 2 Cornish hens, weighing around 500g each
- 2 tbsp olive oil
- 1 tsp garlic powder
- 1 tsp paprika
- 1.5 tsp Italian seasoning
- 1 tbsp lemon juice
- Salt and pepper to taste

Directions:

1. Preheat your air fryer to 260ºC
2. Combine all the ingredients into a bowl (except for the hens) until smooth
3. Brush the hens with the mixture, coating evenly
4. Place in the air fryer basket, with the breast side facing down
5. Cook for 35 minutes
6. Turn over and cook for another 10 minutes
7. Ensure the hens are white in the middle before serving

Honey Cajun Chicken Thighs

Servings: 6
Cooking Time:xx
Ingredients:

- 100ml buttermilk
- 1 tsp hot sauce
- 400g skinless, boneless chicken thighs
- 150g all purpose flour
- 60g tapioca flour
- 2.5 tsp cajun seasoning
- ½ tsp garlic salt
- ½ tsp honey powder
- ¼ tsp ground paprika
- ⅛ tsp cayenne pepper
- 4 tsp honey

Directions:

1. Take a large bowl and combine the buttermilk and hot sauce
2. Transfer to a plastic bag and add the chicken thighs
3. Allow to marinate for 30 minutes
4. Take another bowl and add the flour, tapioca flour, cajun seasoning, garlic, salt, honey powder, paprika, and cayenne pepper, combining well
5. Dredge the chicken through the mixture
6. Preheat the air fryer to 175C
7. Cook for 15 minutes before flipping the thighs over and cooking for another 10 minutes
8. Drizzle 1 tsp of honey over each thigh

Beef & Lamb And Pork Recipes

Asparagus & Steak Parcels

Servings: 4
Cooking Time:xx
Ingredients:

- 500g flank steak, cut into 6 equal pieces
- 75ml Tamari sauce
- 2 crushed garlic cloves
- 250g trimmed asparagus
- 3 large bell peppers, thinly sliced
- 2 tbsp butter
- Salt and pepper to taste

Directions:

1. Season the steak to your liking
2. Place the meat in a zip top bag and add the Tamari and garlic, sealing the bag closed
3. Make sure the steaks are fully coated in the sauce and leave them in the fright at least 1 hour, but preferably overnight
4. Remove the steaks from the bag and throw the marinade away
5. Place the peppers and sliced asparagus in the centre of each steak piece
6. Roll the steak up and secure in place with a tooth pick
7. Preheat your air fryer to 250ºC
8. Transfer the meat parcels to the air fryer and cook for 5 minutes
9. Allow to rest before serving
10. Melt the butter in a saucepan, over a medium heat, adding the juices from the air fryer
11. Combine well and keep cooking until thickened
12. Pour the sauce over the steak parcels and season to your liking

Cheesy Meatball Sub

Servings: 2
Cooking Time:xx
Ingredients:

- 8 frozen pork meatballs
- 5 tbsp marinara sauce
- 160g grated parmesan cheese
- 2 sub rolls or hotdog rolls
- 1/4 tsp dried oregano

Directions:

1. Preheat the air fryer to 220ºC
2. Place the meatball in the air fryer and cook for around 10 minutes, turning halfway through
3. Place the marinara sauce in a bowl
4. Add the meatballs to the sauce and coat completely
5. Add the oregano on top and coat once more
6. Take the bread roll and add the mixture inside
7. Top with the cheese
8. Place the meatball sub back in the air fryer and cook for 2 minutes until the bad is toasted and the cheese has melted

Tender Ham Steaks

Servings: 1
Cooking Time:xx

Ingredients:

- 1 ham steak
- 2 tbsp brown sugar
- 1 tsp honey
- 2 tbsp melted butter

Directions:

1. Preheat the air fryer to 220ºC
2. Combine the melted butter and brown sugar until smooth
3. Add the ham to the air fryer and brush both sides with the butter mixture
4. Cook for 12 minutes, turning halfway through and re-brushing the ham
5. Drizzle honey on top before serving

Steak Popcorn Bites

Servings: 4
Cooking Time:xx

Ingredients:

- 500g steak, cut into 1" sized cubes
- 500g potato chips, ridged ones work best
- 100g flour
- 2 beaten eggs
- Salt and pepper to taste

Directions:

1. Place the chips into the food processor and pulse unit you get fine chip crumbs
2. Take a bowl and combine the flour with salt and pepper
3. Add the chips to another bowl and the beaten egg to another bowl
4. Take the steak cubes and dip first in the flour, then the egg and then the chip crumbs
5. Preheat your air fryer to 260ºC
6. Place the steak pieces into the fryer and cook for 9 minutes

Beef And Cheese Empanadas

Servings: 12
Cooking Time:xx

Ingredients:

- 2 tsp oil
- 1 chopped onion
- 1 clove chopped garlic
- 500g minced beef
- Salt and pepper
- 2 tbsp chopped jalapeño
- 2 packs ready made pastry
- 50g grated cheddar cheese
- 50g pepper jack cheese
- 1 egg

Directions:

1. Heat the oil in a pan and fry the onion and garlic until soft
2. Add the meat and jalapeño, season with salt and pepper, and cook until browned
3. Allow the meat to cool
4. Roll out dough as thin as possible and cut into circles, fill with 1 tablespoon of mix, sprinkle with cheese, fold over and seal with the egg
5. Set your fryer to 170ºC and cook for about 12 minutes until golden brown

Mustard Glazed Pork

Servings: 4
Cooking Time:xx
Ingredients:
- 500g pork tenderloin
- 1 tbsp minced garlic
- ¼ tsp salt
- ⅛ tsp cracked black pepper
- 75g yellow mustard
- 3 tbsp brown sugar
- 1 tsp Italian seasoning
- 1 tsp rosemary

Directions:
1. Cut slits into the pork place the minced garlic into the slits, season with the salt and pepper
2. Add the remaining ingredients to a bowl and whisk to combine
3. Rub the mix over the pork and allow to marinate for 2 hours
4. Place in the air fryer and cook at 200ºC for 20 minutes

Pork With Chinese 5 Spice

Servings: 4
Cooking Time:xx
Ingredients:
- 2 pork rounds cut into chunks
- 2 large eggs
- 1 tsp sesame oil
- 200g cornstarch
- 1/4 tsp salt
- ½ tsp pepper
- 3 tbsp canola oil
- 1 tsp Chinese 5 spice

Directions:
1. In a bowl mix the corn starch, salt, pepper and 5 spice
2. Mix the eggs and sesame oil in another bowl
3. Dip the pork into the egg and then cover in the corn starch mix
4. Place in the air fryer and cook at 170ºC for 11-12 minutes, shaking halfway through
5. Serve with sweet and sour sauce

Hamburgers

Servings: 4
Cooking Time:xx
Ingredients:
- 500g minced beef
- 1 grated onion
- Salt and pepper to taste

Directions:
1. Preheat air fryer to 200ºC
2. Place the grated onion and the beef into a bowl and combine together well
3. Divide minced beef into 4 equal portions, form into patties
4. Season with salt and pepper
5. Place in the air fryer and cook for 10 minutes, turnover and cook for a further 3 minutes

Butter Steak & Asparagus

Servings: 6
Cooking Time:xx
Ingredients:

- 500g steak, cut into 6 pieces
- Salt and pepper
- 75g tamari sauce
- 2 cloves crushed garlic
- 400g asparagus
- 3 sliced peppers
- 25g balsamic vinegar
- 50g beef broth
- 2 tbsp butter

Directions:

1. Season steaks with salt and pepper
2. Place steaks in a bowl, add tamari sauce and garlic make sure steaks are covered, leave to marinate for at least 1hr
3. Place steaks on a board, fill with peppers and asparagus, roll the steak around and secure with tooth picks
4. Set your fryer to 200°C and cook for 5 minutes.
5. Whilst cooking heat the broth, butter and balsamic vinegar in a saucepan until thickened
6. Pour over the steaks and serve

Beef Bulgogi Burgers

Servings: 4
Cooking Time:xx
Ingredients:

- 500g minced beef
- 2 tbsp gochujang
- 1 tbsp soy
- 2 tsp minced garlic
- 2 tsp minced ginger
- 2 tsp sugar
- 1 tbsp olive oil
- 1 chopped onion

Directions:

1. Mix all the ingredients in a large bowl, allow to rest for at least 30 minutes in the fridge
2. Divide the meat into four and form into patties
3. Place in the air fryer and cook at 180°C for about 10 minutes
4. Serve in burger buns, if desired

Cheeseburger Egg Rolls

Servings: 4
Cooking Time:xx

Ingredients:

- 400g minced beef
- ¼ tsp garlic powder
- ¼ tsp onion powder
- 1 chopped red pepper
- 1 chopped onion
- 6 dill pickles, chopped
- Salt and pepper
- 3 tbsp grated cheese
- 3 tbsp cream cheese
- 2 tbsp ketchup
- 1 tbsp mustard
- 6 large egg roll wrappers

Directions:

1. Cook the pepper, onion and minced beef in a pan for about 5 minutes
2. Remove from heat and stir in cheese, cream cheese, ketchup and mustard
3. Put the mix into a bowl and stir in the pickles
4. Place ⅙ of the mix in the centre of each wrap, moisten the edges with water roll up the wrap around the mixture and seal
5. Set your fryer to 200ºC and cook for about 7 minutes
6. Turn the sandwich over and cook for another 3 minutes
7. Turn the sandwich out and serve whilst hot
8. Repeat with the other remaining sandwich

Chinese Pork With Pineapple

Servings: 4
Cooking Time:xx

Ingredients:

- 450g pork loin, cubed
- ½ tsp salt
- ½ tsp pepper
- 1 tbsp brown sugar
- 75g fresh coriander, chopped
- 2 tbsp toasted sesame seeds
- ½ pineapple, cubed
- 1 sliced red pepper
- 1 minced clove of garlic
- 1 tsp ginger
- 2 tbsp soy
- 1 tbsp oil

Directions:

1. Season the pork with salt and pepper
2. Add all ingredients to the air fryer
3. Cook at 180ºC for 17 minutes
4. Serve and garnish with coriander and toasted sesame seeds

Buttermilk Pork Chops

Servings: 4
Cooking Time:xx

Ingredients:

- 4 pork chops
- 3 tbsp buttermilk
- 75g flour
- Cooking oil spray
- 1 packet of pork rub
- Salt and pepper to taste

Directions:

1. Rub the chops with the pork rub
2. Place the pork chops in a bowl and drizzle with buttermilk
3. Coat the chops with flour
4. Place in the air fryer and cook at 190ºC for 15 minutes turning halfway

Southern Style Pork Chops

Servings: 4
Cooking Time:xx

Ingredients:

- 4 pork chops
- 3 tbsp buttermilk
- 100g flour
- Salt and pepper to taste
- Pork rub to taste

Directions:

1. Season the pork with pork rub
2. Drizzle with buttermilk
3. Coat in flour until fully covered
4. Place the pork chops in the air fryer, cook at 170ºC for 15 minutes
5. Turnover and cook for a further 10 minutes

Mongolian Beef

Servings: 4
Cooking Time:xx

Ingredients:

- 500g steak
- 25g cornstarch
- 2 tsp vegetable oil
- ½ tsp ginger
- 1 tbsp garlic minced
- 75g soy sauce
- 75g water
- 100g brown sugar

Directions:

1. Slice the steak and coat in corn starch
2. Place in the air fryer and cook at 200ºC for 10 minutes turning halfway
3. Place remaining ingredients in a sauce pan and gently warm
4. When cooked place the steak in a bowl and pour the sauce over

Beef Stirfry

Servings: 2
Cooking Time:xx
Ingredients:

- 500g steak
- 400g broccoli
- 3 peppers, cut into strips
- 1 tbsp ground ginger
- 25ml water
- 1 sliced onion
- 25g hoisin sauce
- 2 tsp minced garlic
- 1 tsp sesame oil
- 1 tbsp soy

Directions:

1. Add sesame oil, hoisin sauce, garlic, soy and water to a bowl and then add the steak, allow to marinate for 20 minutes
2. Mix 1 tbsp of oil with the vegetables and place in the air fryer, cook at 200ºC for about 5 minutes
3. Place the vegetables in a bowl and put aside
4. Add meat to air fryer and cook for 4 minutes, turn and cook for a further 2 minutes
5. Mix the steak with the vegetables and serve with rice

Italian Meatballs

Servings: 12
Cooking Time:xx
Ingredients:

- 2 tbsp olive oil
- 2 tbsp minced shallot
- 3 cloves garlic minced
- 100g panko crumbs
- 35g chopped parsley
- 1 tbsp chopped rosemary
- 60ml milk
- 400g minced pork
- 250g turkey sausage
- 1 egg beaten
- 1 tbsp dijon mustard
- 1 tbsp finely chopped thyme

Directions:

1. Preheat air fryer to 200ºC
2. Heat oil in a pan and cook the garlic and shallot over a medium heat for 1-2 minutes
3. Mix the panko and milk in a bowl and allow to stand for 5 minutes
4. Add all the ingredients to the panko mix and combine well
5. Shape into 1 ½ inch meatballs and cook for 12 minutes

Bbq Ribs

Servings: 2
Cooking Time:xx
Ingredients:

- 500g ribs
- 3 chopped garlic cloves
- 4 tbsp bbq sauce
- 1 tbsp honey
- ½ tsp five spice
- 1 tsp sesame oil
- 1 tsp salt
- 1 tsp black pepper
- 1 tsp soy sauce

Directions:

1. Chop the ribs into small pieces and place them in a bowl
2. Add all the ingredients into the bowl and mix well
3. Marinate for 4 hours
4. Preheat the air fryer to 180ºC
5. Place the ribs into the air fryer and cook for 15 minutes
6. Coat the ribs in honey and cook for a further 15 minutes

Carne Asada Chips

Servings: 2
Cooking Time:xx
Ingredients:

- 500g sirloin steak
- 1 bag of frozen French fries
- 350g grated cheese
- 2 tbsp sour cream
- 2 tbsp guacamole
- 2 tbsp steak seasoning
- Salt and pepper to taste

Directions:

1. Preheat your oven to 260ºC
2. Season the steak with the seasoning and a little salt and pepper
3. Place in the air fryer and cook for 4 minutes, before turning over and cooking for another 4 minutes
4. Remove and allow to rest
5. Add the French fries to the fryer and cook for 5 minutes, shaking regularly
6. Add the cheese
7. Cut the steak into pieces and add on top of the cheese
8. Cook for another 30 seconds, until the cheese is melted
9. Season

Pork Chilli Cheese Dogs

Servings: 2

Cooking Time:xx

Ingredients:

- 1 can of pork chilli, or chilli you have left over
- 200g grated cheese
- 2 hot dog bread rolls
- 2 hot dogs

Directions:

1. Preheat the air fryer to 260°C
2. Cook the hot dogs for 4 minutes, turning halfway
3. Place the hotdogs inside the bread rolls and place back inside the air fryer
4. Top with half the cheese on top and then the chilli
5. Add the rest of the cheese
6. Cook for an extra 2 minutes

Chinese Chilli Beef

Servings: 2

Cooking Time:xx

Ingredients:

- 4 tbsp light soy sauce
- 1 tsp honey
- 3 tbsp tomato ketchup
- 1 tsp Chinese 5 spice
- 1 tbsp oil
- 6 tbsp sweet chilli sauce
- 1 tbsp lemon juice
- 400g frying steak
- 2 tbsp cornflour

Directions:

1. Slice the steak into strips, put into a bowl and cover with cornflour and 5 spice
2. Add to the air fryer and cook for 6 minutes at 200°C
3. Whilst the beef is cooking mix together the remaining ingredients
4. Add to the air fryer and cook for another 3 minutes

Japanese Pork Chops

Servings: 4

Cooking Time:xx

Ingredients:

- 6 boneless pork chops
- 30g flour
- 2 beaten eggs
- 2 tbsp sweet chilli sauce
- 500g cup seasoned breadcrumbs
- ⅛ tsp salt
- ⅛ tsp pepper
- Tonkatsu sauce to taste

Directions:

1. Place the flour, breadcrumbs and eggs in 3 separate bowls
2. Sprinkle both sides of the pork with salt and pepper
3. Coat the pork in flour, egg and then breadcrumbs
4. Place in the air fryer and cook at 180°C for 8 minutes, turn then cook for a further 5 minutes
5. Serve with sauces on the side

Fish & Seafood Recipes

Salmon Patties

Servings: 4
Cooking Time:xx
Ingredients:
- 400g salmon
- 1 egg
- 1 diced onion
- 200g breadcrumbs
- 1 tsp dill weed

Directions:
1. Remove all bones and skin from the salmon
2. Mix egg, onion, dill weed and bread crumbs with the salmon
3. Shape mixture into patties and place into the air fryer
4. Set air fryer to 180ºC
5. Cook for 5 minutes then turn them over and cook for a further 5 minutes until golden brown

Pesto Salmon

Servings: 4
Cooking Time:xx
Ingredients:
- 4 x 150–175-g/5½–6-oz. salmon fillets
- lemon wedges, to serve
- PESTO
- 50 g/scant ½ cup toasted pine nuts
- 50 g/2 oz. fresh basil
- 50 g/⅔ cup grated Parmesan or Pecorino
- 100 ml/7 tablespoons olive oil

Directions:
1. To make the pesto, blitz the pine nuts, basil and Parmesan to a paste in a food processor. Pour in the olive oil and process again.
2. Preheat the air-fryer to 160ºC/325ºF.
3. Top each salmon fillet with 2 tablespoons of the pesto. Add the salmon fillets to the preheated air-fryer and air-fry for 9 minutes. Check the internal temperature of the fish has reached at least 63ºC/145ºF using a meat thermometer – if not, cook for another few minutes.

Fish Sticks With Tartar Sauce Batter

Servings: 4
Cooking Time:xx
Ingredients:
- 6 tbsp mayonnaise
- 2 tbsp dill pickle
- 1 tsp seafood seasoning
- 400g cod fillets, cut into sticks
- 300g panko breadcrumbs

Directions:
1. Combine the mayonnaise, seafood seasoning and dill pickle in a large bowl.
2. Add the cod sticks and coat well
3. Preheat air fryer to 200ºC
4. Coat the fish sticks in the breadcrumbs
5. Place in the air fryer and cook for 12 minutes

Copycat Fish Fingers

Servings: 2

Cooking Time:xx

Ingredients:

- 2 slices wholemeal bread, grated into breadcrumbs
- 50g plain flour
- 1 beaten egg
- 1 white fish fillet
- The juice of 1 small lemon
- 1 tsp parsley
- 1 tsp thyme
- 1 tsp mixed herbs
- Salt and pepper to taste

Directions:

1. Preheat the air fryer to 180°C
2. Add salt pepper and parsley to the breadcrumbs and combine well
3. Place the egg in another bowl
4. Place the flour in a separate bowl
5. Place the fish into a food processor and add the lemon juice, salt, pepper thyme and mixed herbs
6. Blitz to create a crumb-like consistency
7. Roll your fish in the flour, then the egg and then the breadcrumbs
8. Cook at 180°C for 8 minutes

Air Fryer Tuna

Servings: 2

Cooking Time:xx

Ingredients:

- 2 tuna steaks, boneless and skinless
- 2 tsp honey
- 1 tsp grated ginger
- 4 tbsp soy sauce
- 1 tsp sesame oil
- 1/2 tsp rice vinegar

Directions:

1. Combine the honey, soy sauce, rice vinegar and sesame oil in a bowl until totally mixed together
2. Cover the tuna steaks with the sauce and place in the refrigerator for half an hour to marinade
3. Preheat the air fryer to 270°C
4. Cook the tuna for 4 minutes
5. Allow to rest before slicing

Extra Crispy Popcorn Shrimp

Servings: 2

Cooking Time:xx

Ingredients:

- 300g Frozen popcorn shrimp
- 1 tsp cayenne pepper
- Salt and pepper for seasoning

Directions:

1. Preheat the air fryer to 220°C
2. Place the shrimp inside the air fryer and cook for 6 minutes, giving them a shake at the halfway point
3. Remove and season with salt and pepper, and the cayenne to your liking

Peppery Lemon Shrimp

Servings: 2
Cooking Time:xx
Ingredients:
- 300g uncooked shrimp
- 1 tbsp olive oil
- 1 the juice of 1 lemon
- 0.25 tsp garlic powder
- 1 sliced lemon
- 1 tsp pepper
- 0.25 tsp paprika

Directions:
1. Heat the fryer to 200ºC
2. Take a medium sized mixing bowl and combine the lemon juice, pepper, garlic powder, paprika and the olive oil together
3. Add the shrimp to the bowl and make sure they're well coated
4. Arrange the shrimp into the basket of the fryer
5. Cook for between 6-8 minutes, until firm and pink

Shrimp Wrapped With Bacon

Servings: 2
Cooking Time:xx
Ingredients:
- 16 shrimp
- 16 slices of bacon
- 2 tbsp ranch dressing to serve

Directions:
1. Preheat the air fryer to 200ºC
2. Wrap the shrimps in the bacon
3. Refrigerate for 30 minutes
4. Cook the shrimp for about 5 minutes turn them over and cook for a further 2 minutes
5. Serve with the ranch dressing on the side

Baked Panko Cod

Servings: 5
Cooking Time:xx
Ingredients:
- 400g cod, cut into 5 pieces
- 250g panko breadcrumbs
- 1 egg plus 1 egg white extra
- Cooking spray
- ½ tsp onion powder
- ½ tsp garlic salt
- ⅛ tsp black pepper
- ½ tsp mixed herbs

Directions:
1. Heat air fryer to 220ºC
2. Beat the egg and egg white in a bowl
3. Sprinkle fish with herbs and spice mix, dip into the egg and then cover in the panko bread crumbs
4. Line air fryer basket with tin foil. Place the fish in the air fryer and coat with cooking spray
5. Cook for about 15 minutes until, fish is lightly browned

Cod In Parma Ham

Servings: 2

Cooking Time:xx

Ingredients:

- 2 x 175–190-g/6–7-oz. cod fillets, skin removed
- 6 slices Parma ham or prosciutto
- 16 cherry tomatoes
- 60 g/2 oz. rocket/arugula
- DRESSING
- 1 tablespoon olive oil
- 1½ teaspoons balsamic vinegar
- garlic salt, to taste
- freshly ground black pepper, to taste

Directions:

1. Preheat the air-fryer to 180ºC/350ºF.
2. Wrap each piece of cod snugly in 3 ham slices. Add the ham-wrapped cod fillets and the tomatoes to the preheated air-fryer and air-fry for 6 minutes, turning the cod halfway through cooking. Check the internal temperature of the fish has reached at least 60ºC/140ºF using a meat thermometer – if not, cook for another minute.
3. Meanwhile, make the dressing by combining all the ingredients in a jar and shaking well.
4. Serve the cod and tomatoes on a bed of rocket/arugula with the dressing poured over.

Tilapia Fillets

Servings: 2

Cooking Time:xx

Ingredients:

- 2 tbsp melted butter
- 150g almond flour
- 3 tbsp mayonnaise
- 2tilapia fillets
- 25g thinly sliced almonds
- Salt and pepper to taste
- Vegetable oil spray

Directions:

1. Mix the almond flour, butter, pepper and salt together in a bowl
2. Spread mayonnaise on both sides of the fish
3. Cover the fillets in the almond flour mix
4. Spread one side of the fish with the sliced almonds
5. Spray the air fryer with the vegetable spray
6. Place in the air fryer and cook at 160ºC for 10 minutes

Thai-style Tuna Fishcakes

Servings: 2
Cooking Time:xx

Ingredients:

- 200 g/7 oz. cooked potato
- 145 g/5 oz. canned tuna, drained
- 60 g/1 cup canned sweetcorn/corn kernels (drained weight)
- ½ teaspoon soy sauce
- ½ teaspoon fish sauce
- ½ teaspoon Thai 7 spice
- freshly squeezed juice of ½ a lime
- 1 teaspoon freshly grated garlic
- 1 teaspoon freshly grated ginger
- avocado or olive oil, for brushing
- LIME-ALMOND SATAY SAUCE
- 20 ml/4 teaspoons fresh lime juice
- 2 heaped tablespoons almond butter
- 1 teaspoon soy sauce
- ½ teaspoon freshly grated ginger
- ½ teaspoon freshly grated garlic
- ½ teaspoon avocado or olive oil
- ½ teaspoon maple syrup

Directions:

1. Combine all the fishcake ingredients in a food processor and blend together. Divide the mixture into 6 equal portions and mould into fishcakes. Brush a little oil over the top surface of the fishcakes.
2. Preheat the air-fryer to 180°C/350°F.
3. Place the fishcakes on an air-fryer liner or a piece of pierced parchment paper and add to the preheated air-fryer. Air-fry for 4 minutes, then turn over and brush the other side of each fishcake with oil and air-fry for a further 4 minutes.
4. To make the satay dipping sauce, mix all ingredients in a bowl with 1 tablespoon warm water. Serve alongside the fishcakes.

Crunchy Fish

Servings: 4
Cooking Time:xx

Ingredients:

- 200g dry breadcrumbs
- 4 tbsp olive oil
- 4 fillets of white fish
- 1 beaten egg
- 1 sliced lemon

Directions:

1. Heat the fryer to 180°C
2. In a medium mixing bowl, combine the olive oil and the breadcrumbs
3. Take the fish and first dip it into the egg and then the breadcrumbs, making sure they are evenly coated well
4. Arrange the fish into the basket
5. Cook for 12 minutes
6. Remove and serve with lemon slices

Garlic Tilapia

Servings: 2

Cooking Time:xx

Ingredients:

- 2 tilapia fillets
- 2 tsp chopped fresh chives
- 2 tsp chopped fresh parsley
- 2 tsp olive oil
- 1 tsp minced garlic
- Salt and pepper for seasoning

Directions:

1. Preheat the air fryer to 220ºC
2. Take a small bowl and combine the olive oil with the chives, garlic, parsley and a little salt and pepper
3. Brush the mixture over the fish fillets
4. Place the fish into the air fryer and cook for 10 minutes, until flaky

Fish In Parchment Paper

Servings: 2

Cooking Time:xx

Ingredients:

- 250g cod fillets
- 1 chopped carrot
- 1 chopped fennel
- 1 tbsp oil
- 1 thinly sliced red pepper
- ½ tsp tarragon
- 1 tbsp lemon juice
- 1 tbsp salt
- ½ tsp ground pepper

Directions:

1. In a bowl, mix the tarragon and ½ tsp salt add the vegetables and mix well
2. Cut two large squares of parchment paper
3. Spray the cod with oil and cover both sides with salt and pepper
4. Place the cod in the parchment paper and add the vegetables
5. Fold over the paper to hold the fish and vegetables
6. Place in the air fryer and cook at 170ºC for 15 minutes

Ranch Style Fish Fillets

Servings: 4

Cooking Time:xx

Ingredients:

- 200g bread crumbs
- 30g ranch-style dressing mix
- 2 tbsp oil
- 2 beaten eggs
- 4 fish fillets of your choice
- Lemon wedges to garnish

Directions:

1. Preheat air fryer to 180ºC
2. Mix the bread crumbs and ranch dressing mix together, add in the oil until the mix becomes crumbly
3. Dip the fish into the, then cover in the breadcrumb mix
4. Place in the air fryer and cook for 12-13 minutes

Parmesan-coated Fish Fingers

Servings: 2
Cooking Time:xx
Ingredients:

- 350 g/12 oz. cod loins
- 1 tablespoon grated Parmesan
- 40 g/½ cup dried breadcrumbs (gluten-free if you wish, see page 9)
- 1 egg, beaten
- 2 tablespoons plain/all-purpose flour (gluten free if you wish)

Directions:

1. Slice the cod into 6 equal fish fingers/sticks.
2. Mix the Parmesan together with the breadcrumbs. Lay out three bowls: one with flour, one with beaten egg and the other with the Parmesan breadcrumbs. Dip each fish finger/stick first into the flour, then the egg and then the breadcrumbs until fully coated.
3. Preheat the air-fryer to 180ºC/350ºF.
4. Add the fish to the preheated air-fryer and air-fry for 6 minutes. Check the internal temperature of the fish has reached at least 75ºC/167ºF using a meat thermometer – if not, cook for another few minutes. Serve immediately.

Cajun Shrimp Boil

Servings: 6
Cooking Time:xx
Ingredients:

- 300g cooked shrimp
- 14 slices of smoked sausage
- 5 par boiled potatoes, cut into halves
- 4 mini corn on the cobs, quartered
- 1 diced onion
- 3 tbsp old bay seasoning
- Olive oil spray

Directions:

1. Combine all the ingredients in a bowl and mix well
2. Line the air fryer with foil
3. Place half the mix into the air fryer and cook at 200ºC for about 6 minutes, mix the ingredients and cook for a further 6 minutes.
4. Repeat for the second batch

Air Fryer Mussels

Servings: 2
Cooking Time:xx
Ingredients:

- 400g mussels
- 1 tbsp butter
- 200ml water
- 1 tsp basil
- 2 tsp minced garlic
- 1 tsp chives
- 1 tsp parsley

Directions:

1. Preheat air fryer to 200ºC
2. Clean the mussels, soak for 30 minutes, and remove the beard
3. Add all ingredients to an air fryer-safe pan
4. Cook for 3 minutes
5. Check to see if the mussels have opened, if not cook for a further 2 minutes. Once all mussels are open, they are ready to eat.

Crispy Nacho Prawns

Servings: 6
Cooking Time:xx

Ingredients:

- 1 egg
- 18 large prawns
- 1 bag of nacho cheese flavoured corn chips, crushed

Directions:

1. Wash the prawns and pat dry
2. Place the chips into a bowl
3. In another bowl, whisk the egg
4. Dip the prawns into the egg and then the nachos
5. Preheat the air fryer to 180ºC
6. Cook for 8 minutes

Garlic-parsley Prawns

Servings: 2
Cooking Time:xx

Ingredients:

- 300 g/10½ oz. raw king prawns/jumbo shrimp (without shell)
- 40 g/3 tablespoons garlic butter, softened (see page 72)
- 2 tablespoons freshly chopped flat-leaf parsley

Directions:

1. Thread the prawns/shrimp onto 6 metal skewers that will fit your air-fryer. Mix together the softened garlic butter and parsley and brush evenly onto the prawn skewers.
2. Preheat the air-fryer to 180ºC/350ºF.
3. Place the skewers on an air-fryer liner or a piece of pierced parchment paper. Add the skewers to the preheated air-fryer and air-fry for 2 minutes, then turn the skewers over and cook for a further 2 minutes. Check the internal temperature of the prawns has reached at least 50ºC/120ºF using a meat thermometer – if not, cook for another few minutes and serve.

Gluten Free Honey And Garlic Shrimp

Servings: 2
Cooking Time:xx

Ingredients:

- 500g fresh shrimp
- 5 tbsp honey
- 2 tbsp gluten free soy sauce
- 2 tbsp tomato ketchup
- 250g frozen stir fry vegetables
- 1 crushed garlic clove
- 1 tsp fresh ginger
- 2 tbsp cornstarch

Directions:

1. Simmer the honey, soy sauce, garlic, tomato ketchup and ginger in a saucepan
2. Add the cornstarch and whisk until sauce thickens
3. Coat the shrimp with the sauce
4. Line the air fryer with foil and add the shrimp and vegetables
5. Cook at 180ºC for 10 minutes

Vegetarian & Vegan Recipes

Vegan Fried Ravioli

Servings: 4
Cooking Time:xx
Ingredients:

- 100g panko breadcrumbs
- 2 tsp yeast
- 1 tsp basil
- 1 tsp oregano
- 1 tsp garlic powder
- Pinch salt and pepper
- 50ml liquid from can of chickpeas
- 150g vegan ravioli
- Cooking spray
- 50g marinara for dipping

Directions:

1. Combine the breadcrumbs, yeast, basil, oregano, garlic powder and salt and pepper
2. Put the liquid from the chickpeas in a bowl
3. Dip the ravioli in the liquid then dip into the breadcrumb mix
4. Heat the air fryer to 190ºC
5. Place the ravioli in the air fryer and cook for about 6 minutes until crispy

Vegan Meatballs

Servings:4
Cooking Time:15 Minutes
Ingredients:

- 2 tbsp olive oil
- 2 tbsp soy sauce
- 1 onion, finely sliced
- 1 large carrot, peeled and grated
- 1 x 400 g / 14 oz can chickpeas, drained and rinsed
- 50 g / 1.8 oz plain flour
- 50 g / 1.8 oz rolled oats
- 2 tbsp roasted cashews, chopped
- 1 tsp garlic powder
- ½ tsp cumin

Directions:

1. Preheat the air fryer to 175 °C / 350 °F and line the air fryer with parchment paper or grease it with olive oil.

2. In a large mixing bowl, combine the olive oil and soy sauce. Add the onion slices and grated carrot and toss to coat in the sauce.

3. Place the vegetables in the air fryer and cook for 5 minutes until slightly soft.

4. Meanwhile, place the chickpeas, plain flour, rolled oats, and roasted cashews in a blender, and mix until well combined.

5. Remove the mixture from the blender and stir in the garlic powder and cumin. Add the onions and carrots to the bowl and mix well.

6. Scoop the mixture into small meatballs and place them into the air fryer. Increase the temperature on the machine up to 190 °C / 370 °F and cook the meatballs for 10-12 minutes until golden and crispy.

Roasted Vegetable Pasta

Servings:4
Cooking Time:15 Minutes
Ingredients:

- 400 g / 14 oz penne pasta
- 1 courgette, sliced
- 1 red pepper, deseeded and sliced
- 100 g / 3.5 oz mushroom, sliced
- 2 tbsp olive oil
- 1 tsp Italian seasoning
- 200 g cherry tomatoes, halved
- 2 tbsp fresh basil, chopped
- ½ tsp black pepper

Directions:

1. Cook the pasta according to the packet instructions.
2. Preheat the air fryer to 190 °C / 370 °F and line the air fryer with parchment paper or grease it with olive oil.
3. In a bowl, place the courgette, pepper, and mushroom, and toss in 2 tbsp olive oil
4. Place the vegetables in the air fryer and cook for 15 minutes.
5. Once the vegetables have softened, mix with the penne pasta, chopped cherry tomatoes, and fresh basil.
6. Serve while hot with a sprinkle of black pepper in each dish.

Spring Ratatouille

Servings:2
Cooking Time:15 Minutes
Ingredients:

- 1 tbsp olive oil
- 4 Roma tomatoes, sliced
- 2 cloves garlic, minced
- 1 courgette, cut into chunks
- 1 red pepper and 1 yellow pepper, cut into chunks
- 2 tbsp mixed herbs
- 1 tbsp vinegar

Directions:

1. Preheat the air fryer to 190 °C / 370 °F and line the air fryer with parchment paper or grease it with olive oil.
2. Place all of the ingredients into a large mixing bowl and mix until fully combined.
3. Transfer the vegetables into the lined air fryer basket, close the lid, and cook for 15 minutes until the vegetables have softened.

Roasted Garlic

Servings: 2
Cooking Time:xx
Ingredients:

- 1 head of garlic
- Drizzle of olive oil
- Salt and pepper for seasoning

Directions:

1. Remove paper peel from garlic
2. Place in foil and drizzle with oil
3. Place in the air fryer and cook at 200ºC for 20 minutes
4. Season before serving

Camembert & Soldiers

Servings: 2

Cooking Time:xx

Ingredients:

- 1 piece of Camembert
- 2 slices sandwich bread
- 1 tbsp mustard

Directions:

1. Preheat the air fryer to 180ºC
2. Place the camembert in a sturdy container, cook in the air fryer for 15 minutes
3. Toast the bread and cut into soldiers
4. Serve with the mustard by the side

Courgette Burgers

Servings: 4

Cooking Time:xx

Ingredients:

- 1 courgette
- 1 small can of chickpeas, drained
- 3 spring onions
- Pinch of dried garlic
- Salt and pepper
- 3 tbsp coriander
- 1 tsp chilli powder
- 1 tsp mixed spice
- 1 tsp cumin

Directions:

1. Grate the courgette and drain the excess water
2. Thinly slice the spring onions and add to the bowl with the chickpeas, courgette and seasoning
3. Bind the ingredients and form into patties
4. Place in the air fryer and cook for 12 minutes at 200ºC

Bbq Soy Curls

Servings: 2

Cooking Time:xx

Ingredients:

- 250ml warm water
- 1 tsp vegetable bouillon
- 200g soy curls
- 40g BBQ sauce
- 1 tsp oil

Directions:

1. Soak the soy curls in water and bouillon for 10 minutes
2. Place the soy curls in another bowl and shred
3. Heat the air fryer to 200ºC
4. Cook for 3 minutes
5. Remove from the air fryer and coat in bbq sauce
6. Return to the air fryer and cook for 5 minutes shaking halfway through

Flat Mushroom Pizzas

Servings: 1
Cooking Time:xx
Ingredients:

- 2 portobello mushrooms, cleaned and stalk removed
- 6 mozzarella balls
- 1 teaspoon olive oil
- PIZZA SAUCE
- 100 g/3½ oz. passata/strained tomatoes
- 1 teaspoon dried oregano
- ¼ teaspoon garlic salt

Directions:

1. Preheat the air-fryer to 180ºC/350ºF.
2. Mix the ingredients for the pizza sauce together in a small bowl. Fill each upturned portobello mushroom with sauce, then top each with three mozzarella balls and drizzle the olive oil over.
3. Add the mushrooms to the preheated air-fryer and air-fry for 8 minutes. Serve immediately.

Mini Quiche

Servings: 2
Cooking Time:xx
Ingredients:

- 100g raw cashews
- 3 tbsp milk
- ½ tsp hot sauce
- 1 tsp white miso paste
- 1 tsp mustard
- 300g tofu
- 100g bacon pieces
- 1 chopped red pepper
- 1 chopped onion
- 6 tbsp yeast
- ½ tsp onion powder
- ½ tsp paprika
- ½ tsp cumin
- ½ tsp chilli powder
- ½ tsp black pepper
- ⅛ tsp turmeric
- ½ tsp canola oil
- 50g curly kale

Directions:

1. Heat the oil in a pan, add the bacon pepper, onion and curly kale and cook for about 3 minutes
2. Place all the other ingredients into a blender and blend until smooth
3. Add to a bowl with the bacon, pepper, onion and curly kale and mix well
4. Fill silicone muffin cups with the mix
5. Place in the air fryer and cook at 165ºC for 15 minutes

Miso Mushrooms On Sourdough Toast

Servings: 1

Cooking Time:xx

Ingredients:

- 1 teaspoon miso paste
- 1 teaspoon oil, such as avocado or coconut (melted)
- 1 teaspoon soy sauce
- 80 g/3 oz. chestnut mushrooms, sliced 5 mm/½ in. thick
- 1 large slice sourdough bread
- 2 teaspoons butter or plant-based spread
- a little freshly chopped flat-leaf parsley, to serve

Directions:

1. Preheat the air-fryer to 200ºC/400ºF.
2. In a small bowl or ramekin mix together the miso paste, oil and soy sauce.
3. Place the mushrooms in a small shallow gratin dish that fits inside your air-fryer. Add the sauce to the mushrooms and mix together. Place the gratin dish in the preheated air-fryer and air-fry for 6–7 minutes, stirring once during cooking.
4. With 4 minutes left to cook, add the bread to the air-fryer and turn over at 2 minutes whilst giving the mushrooms a final stir.
5. Once cooked, butter the toast and serve the mushrooms on top, scattered with chopped parsley.

Baked Feta, Tomato & Garlic Pasta

Servings: 2

Cooking Time:xx

Ingredients:

- 100 g/3½ oz. feta or plant-based feta, cubed
- 20 cherry tomatoes
- 2 garlic cloves, peeled and halved
- ¾ teaspoon oregano
- 1 teaspoon chilli/hot red pepper flakes
- ½ teaspoon garlic salt
- 2 tablespoons olive oil
- 100 g/3½ oz. cooked pasta plus about 1 tablespoon of cooking water
- freshly ground black pepper

Directions:

1. Preheat the air-fryer to 200ºC/400ºF.
2. Place the feta, tomatoes and garlic in a baking dish that fits inside your air-fryer. Top with the oregano, chilli/hot red pepper flakes, garlic salt and olive oil. Place the dish in the preheated air-fryer and air-fry for 10 minutes, then remove and stir in the pasta and cooking water. Serve sprinkled with black pepper.

Veggie Bakes

Servings: 2

Cooking Time:xx

Ingredients:

- Any type of leftover vegetable bake you have
- 30g flour

Directions:

1. Preheat the air fryer to 180ºC
2. Mix the flour with the leftover vegetable bake
3. Shape into balls and place in the air fryer
4. Cook for 10 minutes

Sweet Potato Taquitos

Servings: 10

Cooking Time:xx

Ingredients:

- 1 sweet potato cut into ½ inch pieces
- 1 ½ tsp oil
- 1 chopped onion
- 1 tsp minced garlic
- 400g black beans
- 3 tbsp water
- 10 corn tortillas
- 1 chipotle pepper, chopped
- ½ tsp cumin
- ½ tsp paprika
- ½ chilli powder
- ⅛ tsp salt
- ½ tsp maple syrup

Directions:

1. Place the sweet potato in the air fryer spray with oil and cook for 12 minutes at 200ºC
2. Heat oil in a pan, add the onion and garlic and cook for a few minutes until soft
3. Add remaining ingredients to the pan, add 2 tbsp of water and combine
4. Add the sweet potato and 1 tbsp of water and mix
5. Warm the tortilla in the microwave for about 1 minute
6. Place a row of filling across the centre of each tortilla. Fold up the bottom of the tortilla, tuck under the filling, fold in the edges then continue to roll the tortilla
7. Place in the air fryer and cook for about 12 minutes

Chickpea And Sweetcorn Falafel

Servings:4

Cooking Time:15 Minutes

Ingredients:

- ½ onion, sliced
- 2 cloves garlic, peeled and sliced
- 2 tbsp fresh parsley, chopped
- 2 tbsp fresh coriander, chopped
- 2 x 400 g / 14 oz chickpeas, drained and rinsed
- 1 tsp salt
- 1 tsp black pepper
- 1 tsp baking powder
- 1 tsp dried mixed herbs
- 1 tsp cumin
- 1 tsp chili powder
- 50 g / 1.8 oz sweetcorn, fresh or frozen

Directions:

1. Preheat the air fryer to 180 °C / 350 °F and line the bottom of the basket with parchment paper.
2. In a food processor, place the onion, garlic cloves, fresh parsley, and fresh coriander. Pulse the ingredients in 30-second intervals until they form a smooth mixture. Scrape the mixture from the sides of the food processor in between each interval if necessary.
3. Mix in the chickpeas, salt, black pepper, baking powder, dried mixed herbs, cumin, and chili powder. Pulse the mixture until fully combined and smooth. Add more water if the mixture is looking a bit dry. The mixture should be dry but not crumbly.
4. Use a spoon to scoop out 2 tbsp of the chickpea mixture at a time and roll into small, even falafels.
5. Transfer the falafels into the prepared air fryer basket and cook for 12-15 minutes.
6. Serve the falafels either hot or cold as a side dish to your main meal or as part of a large salad.

Bagel Pizza

Servings: 1
Cooking Time:xx
Ingredients:

- 1 bagel
- 2 tbsp marinara sauce
- 6 slices vegan pepperoni
- 2 tbsp mozzarella
- Pinch of basil

Directions:

1. Heat the air fryer to 180ºC
2. Cut the bagel in half and toast for 2 minutes in the air fryer
3. Remove from the air fryer and top with marinara sauce, pepperoni and mozzarella
4. Return to the air fryer and cook for 4-5 minutes
5. Sprinkle with basil to serve

Aubergine Dip

Servings: 4
Cooking Time:xx
Ingredients:

- 1 aubergine
- 2 tsp oil
- 3 tbsp tahini
- 1 tbsp lemon juice
- 1 clove garlic minced
- ⅛ tsp cumin
- ¼ tsp smoked salt
- ⅛ tsp salt
- Drizzle olive oil

Directions:

1. Cut the aubergine in half length wise and coat in oil, Place in the air fryer and cook at 200ºC for 20 minutes
2. Remove from the air fryer and allow to cool
3. Scoop out the aubergine from the peel and put in a food processor
4. Add all the remaining ingredients, blend to combine but not to a puree
5. Serve with a drizzle of olive oil

Paneer Tikka

Servings: 2
Cooking Time:xx
Ingredients:

- 200ml yogurt
- 1 tsp ginger garlic paste
- 1 tsp red chilli powder
- 1 tsp garam masala
- 1 tsp turmeric powder
- 1 tbsp dried fenugreek leaves
- The juice of 1 lemon
- 2 tbsp chopped coriander
- 1 tbsp olive oil
- 250g paneer cheese, cut into cubes
- 1 green pepper, chopped
- 1 red pepper, chopped
- 1 yellow pepper, chopped
- 1 chopped onion

Directions:

1. Take a mixing bowl and add the yogurt, garlic paste, red chilli powder, garam masala, turmeric powder, lemon juice, fenugreek and chopped coriander, combining well
2. Place the marinade to one side
3. Add the cubed cheese to the marinade and toss to coat well
4. Leave to marinade for 2 hours
5. Take 8 skewers and alternate the cheese with the peppers and onions
6. Drizzle a little oil over the top
7. Arrange in the air fryer and cook at 220ºC for 3 minutes
8. Turn and cook for another 3 minutes

Spinach And Egg Air Fryer Breakfast Muffins

Servings:4

Cooking Time:10 Minutes

Ingredients:

- 8 eggs
- 100 g / 3.5 oz fresh spinach
- 50 g / 1.8 oz cheddar cheese, grated
- ½ onion, finely sliced
- 1 tsp black pepper

Directions:

1. Preheat your air fryer to 200 °C / 400 °F and line an 8-pan muffin tray with parchment paper or grease with olive oil.
2. Gently press the spinach leaves into the bottom of each prepared muffin cup.
3. Sprinkle the finely sliced onion on top of the spinach.
4. Crack 2 eggs into each cup on top of the spinach and add some of the grated cheddar cheese on top of the eggs. Top with a light sprinkle of black pepper.
5. Carefully place the muffins into the air fryer basket and shut the lid. Bake for 10 minutes until the eggs are set and the muffins are hot throughout.
6. Serve the muffins while still hot for breakfast.

Baked Aubergine Slices With Yogurt Dressing

Servings: 2

Cooking Time:xx

Ingredients:

- 1 aubergine/eggplant, sliced 1.5 cm/⅝ in. thick
- 3 tablespoons olive oil
- ½ teaspoon salt
- YOGURT DRESSING
- 1 small garlic clove
- 1 tablespoon tahini or nut butter
- 100 g/½ cup Greek yogurt
- 2 teaspoons freshly squeezed lemon juice
- 1 tablespoon runny honey
- a pinch of salt
- a pinch of ground cumin
- a pinch of sumac
- TO SERVE
- 30 g/1 oz. rocket/arugula
- 2 tablespoons freshly chopped mint
- 3 tablespoons pomegranate seeds

Directions:

1. Preheat the air-fryer to 180ºC/350ºF.
2. Drizzle the olive oil over each side of the aubergine/eggplant slices. Sprinkle with salt. Add the aubergines to the preheated air-fryer and air-fry for 10 minutes, turning halfway through cooking.
3. Meanwhile, make the dressing by combining all the ingredients in a mini food processor (alterantively, finely chop the garlic, add to a jar with the other ingredients and shake vigorously).
4. Serve the cooked aubergine slices on a bed of rocket/arugula, drizzled with the dressing and with the mint and pomegranate seeds scattered over the top.

Ratatouille

Servings: 4
Cooking Time:xx

Ingredients:

- ½ small aubergine, cubed
- 1 courgette, cubed
- 1 tomato, cubed
- 1 pepper, cut into cubes
- ½ onion, diced
- 1 fresh cayenne pepper, sliced
- 1 tsp vinegar
- 5 sprigs basil, chopped
- 2 sprigs oregano, chopped
- 1 clove garlic, crushed
- Salt and pepper
- 1 tbsp olive oil
- 1 tbsp white wine

Directions:

1. Preheat air fryer to 200ºC
2. Place all ingredients in a bowl and mix
3. Pour into a baking dish
4. Add dish to the air fryer and cook for 8 minutes, stir then cook for another 10 minutes

Ravioli Air Fryer Style

Servings: 4
Cooking Time:xx

Ingredients:

- Half a pack of frozen ravioli
- 200g Italian breadcrumbs
- 200ml buttermilk
- 5 tbsp marinara sauce
- 1 tbsp olive oil

Directions:

1. Preheat the air fryer to 220ºC
2. Place the buttermilk in a bowl
3. Add the breadcrumbs to another bowl
4. Take each piece of ravioli and dip it first into the buttermilk and then into the breadcrumbs, coating evenly
5. Add the ravioli to the air fryer and cook for 7 minutes, adding a small amount of oil at the halfway point
6. Serve with the marinara sauce on the side

Side Dishes Recipes

<u>Stuffed Jacket Potatoes</u>

Servings: 4
Cooking Time:xx
Ingredients:

- 2 large russet potatoes
- 2 tsp olive oil
- 100ml yoghurt
- 100ml milk
- ¼ tsp pepper
- 50g chopped spinach
- 2 tbsp nutritional yeast
- ½ tsp salt

Directions:

1. Preheat the air fryer to 190°C
2. Rub the potatoes with oil
3. Place the potatoes in the air fryer and cook for 30 minutes, turn and cook for a further 30 minutes
4. Cut each potato in half and scoop out the middles, mash with yoghurt, milk and yeast. Stir in the spinach and season with salt and pepper
5. Add the mix back into the potato skins and place in the air fryer, cook at 160°C for about 5 mins

Onion Rings

Servings: 4
Cooking Time:xx
Ingredients:

- 200g flour
- 75g cornstarch
- 2 tsp baking powder
- 1 tsp salt
- 2 pinches of paprika
- 1 large onion, cut into rings
- 1 egg
- 1 cup milk
- 200g breadcrumbs
- 2 pinches garlic powder

Directions:

1. Stir flour, salt, starch and baking powder together in a bowl
2. Dip onion rings into the flour mix to coat
3. Whisk the egg and milk into the flour mix, dip in the onion rings
4. Dip the onion rings into the bread crumbs
5. Heat the air fryer to 200°C
6. Place the onion rings in the air fryer and cook for 2-3 minutes until golden brown
7. Sprinkle with paprika and garlic powder to serve

Cheesy Garlic Asparagus

Servings: 4
Cooking Time:xx

Ingredients:

- 1 tsp olive oil
- 500g asparagus
- 1 tsp garlic salt
- 1 tbsp grated parmesan cheese
- Salt and pepper for seasoning

Directions:

1. Preheat the air fryer to 270ºC
2. Clean the asparagus and cut off the bottom 1"
3. Pat dry and place in the air fryer, covering with the oil
4. Sprinkle the parmesan and garlic salt on top, seasoning to your liking
5. Cook for between 7 and 10 minutes
6. Add a little extra parmesan over the top before serving

Alternative Stuffed Potatoes

Servings: 4
Cooking Time:xx

Ingredients:

- 4 baking potatoes, peeled and halved
- 1 tbsp olive oil
- 150g grated cheese
- ½ onion, diced
- 2 slices bacon

Directions:

1. Preheat air fryer to 175ºC
2. Brush the potatoes with oil and cook in the air fryer for 10 minutes
3. Coat again with oil and cook for a further 10 minutes
4. Cut the potatoes in half spoon the insides into a bowl and mix in the cheese
5. Place the bacon and onion in a pan and cook until browned, mix in with the potato
6. Stuff the skins with the mix and return to the air fryer, cook for about 6 minutes

Whole Sweet Potatoes

Servings: 4 As A Side Or Snack
Cooking Time:xx

Ingredients:

- 4 medium sweet potatoes
- 1 tablespoon olive oil
- 1 teaspoon salt
- toppings of your choice

Directions:

1. Preheat the air-fryer to 200ºC/400ºF.
2. Wash and remove any imperfections from the skin of the sweet potatoes, then rub the potatoes with the olive oil and salt.
3. Add the sweet potatoes to the preheated air-fryer and air-fry for up to 40 minutes (the cooking time depends on the size of the potatoes). Remove as soon as they are soft when pierced. Slice open and serve with your choice of toppings.
4. VARIATION: WHOLE JACKET POTATOES
5. Regular baking potatoes can be air-fried in the same way, but will require a cooking time of 45–60 minutes, depending on their size.

Zingy Roasted Carrots

Servings: 4
Cooking Time:xx
Ingredients:

- 500g carrots
- 1 tsp olive oil
- 1 tsp cayenne pepper
- Salt and pepper for seasoning

Directions:

1. Peel the carrots and cut them into chunks, around 2" in size
2. Preheat your air fryer to 220ºC
3. Add the carrots to a bowl with the olive oil and cayenne and toss to coat
4. Place in the fryer and cook for 15 minutes, giving them a stir halfway through
5. Season before serving

Asparagus Spears

Servings: 2
Cooking Time:xx
Ingredients:

- 1 bunch of trimmed asparagus
- 1 teaspoon olive oil
- ¼ teaspoon salt
- ⅛ teaspoon freshly ground black pepper

Directions:

1. Preheat the air-fryer to 180ºC/350ºF.
2. Toss the asparagus spears in the oil and seasoning. Add these to the preheated air-fryer and air-fry for 8–12 minutes, turning once (cooking time depends on the thickness of the stalks, which should retain some bite).

Cauliflower With Hot Sauce And Blue Cheese Sauce

Servings:2
Cooking Time:15 Minutes
Ingredients:

- For the cauliflower:
- 1 cauliflower, broken into florets
- 4 tbsp hot sauce
- 2 tbsp olive oil
- 1 tsp garlic powder
- ½ tsp salt
- ½ tsp black pepper
- 1 tbsp plain flour
- 1 tbsp corn starch
- For the blue cheese sauce:
- 50 g / 1.8 oz blue cheese, crumbled
- 2 tbsp sour cream
- 2 tbsp mayonnaise
- ½ tsp salt
- ½ tsp black pepper

Directions:

1. Preheat the air fryer to 180 °C / 350 °F and line the bottom of the basket with parchment paper.
2. In a bowl, combine the hot sauce, olive oil, garlic powder, salt, and black pepper until it forms a consistent mixture. Add the cauliflower to the bowl and coat in the sauce.
3. Stir in the plain flour and corn starch until well combined.
4. Transfer the cauliflower to the lined basket in the air fryer, close the lid, and cook for 12-15 minutes until the cauliflower has softened and is golden in colour.
5. Meanwhile, make the blue cheese sauce by combining all of the ingredients. When the cauliflower is ready, remove it from the air fryer and serve with the blue cheese sauce on the side.

Spicy Green Beans

Servings: 4

Cooking Time:xx

Ingredients:

- 300g green beans
- 1 tbsp sesame oil
- 1 tsp soy
- 1 tsp rice wine vinegar
- 1 clove garlic, minced
- 1 tsp red pepper flakes

Directions:

1. Preheat air fryer to 200ºC
2. Place green beans in a bowl
3. Mix together remaining ingredients, add green beans and fully coat
4. Place in the air fryer and cook for 12 minutes

Corn On The Cob

Servings: 4

Cooking Time:xx

Ingredients:

- 75g mayo
- 2 tsp grated cheese
- 1 tsp lime juice
- ¼ tsp chilli powder
- 2 ears of corn, cut into 4

Directions:

1. Heat the air fryer to 200ºC
2. Mix the mayo, cheese lime juice and chilli powder in a bowl
3. Cover the corn in the mayo mix
4. Place in the air fryer and cook for 8 minutes

Mexican Rice

Servings: 4

Cooking Time:xx

Ingredients:

- 500g long grain rice
- 3 tbsp olive oil
- 60ml water
- 1 tsp chilli powder
- 1/4 tsp cumin
- 2 tbsp tomato paste
- 1/2 tsp garlic powder
- 1tsp red pepper flakes
- 1 chopped onion
- 500ml chicken stock
- Half a small jalapeño pepper with seeds out, chopped
- Salt for seasoning

Directions:

1. Add the water and tomato paste and combine, placing to one side
2. Take a baking pan and add a little oil
3. Wash the rice and add to the baking pan
4. Add the chicken stock, tomato paste, jalapeños, onions, and the rest of the olive oil, and combine
5. Place aluminium foil over the top and place in your air fryer
6. Cook at 220ºC for 50 minutes
7. Keep checking the rice as it cooks, as the liquid should be absorbing

Sweet Potato Wedges

Servings:4
Cooking Time:20 Minutes
Ingredients:

- ½ tsp garlic powder
- ½ tsp cumin
- ½ tsp smoked paprika
- ½ tsp cayenne pepper
- ½ tsp salt
- ½ tsp black pepper
- 1 tsp dried chives
- 4 tbsp olive oil
- 3 large sweet potatoes, cut into wedges

Directions:

1. Preheat the air fryer to 180 °C / 350 °F and line the bottom of the basket with parchment paper.
2. In a bowl, mix the garlic powder, cumin, smoked paprika, cayenne pepper, salt, black pepper, and dried chives until combined.
3. Whisk in the olive oil and coat the sweet potato wedges in the spicy oil mixture.
4. Transfer the coated sweet potatoes to the air fryer and close the lid. Cook for 20 minutes until cooked and crispy. Serve hot as a side with your main meal.

Pumpkin Fries

Servings: 4
Cooking Time:xx
Ingredients:

- 1 small pumpkin, seeds removed and peeled, cut into half inch slices
- 2 tsp olive oil
- 1 tsp garlic powder
- 1/2 tsp paprika
- A pinch of salt

Directions:

1. Take a large bowl and add the slices of pumpkin
2. Add the oil and all the seasonings. Toss to coat well
3. Place in the air fryer
4. Cook at 280ºC for 15 minutes, until the chips are tender, shaking at the halfway point

Potato Hay

Servings: 4
Cooking Time:xx
Ingredients:

- 2 potatoes
- 1 tbsp oil
- Salt and pepper to taste

Directions:

1. Cut the potatoes into spirals
2. Soak in a bowl of water for 20 minutes, drain and pat dry
3. Add oil, salt and pepper and mix well to coat
4. Preheat air fryer to 180ºC
5. Add potatoes to air fryer and cook for 5 minutes, toss then cook for another 12 until golden brown

Celery Root Fries

Servings: 2
Cooking Time:xx
Ingredients:

- ½ celeriac, cut into sticks
- 500ml water
- 1 tbsp lime juice
- 1 tbsp olive oil
- 75g mayo
- 1 tbsp mustard
- 1 tbsp powdered horseradish

Directions:

1. Put celeriac in a bowl, add water and lime juice, soak for 30 minutes
2. Preheat air fryer to 200
3. Mix together the mayo, horseradish powder and mustard, refrigerate
4. Drain the celeriac, drizzle with oil and season with salt and pepper
5. Place in the air fryer and cook for about 10 minutes turning halfway
6. Serve with the mayo mix as a dip

Potato Wedges With Rosemary

Servings: 2
Cooking Time:xx
Ingredients:

- 2 potatoes, sliced into wedges
- 1 tbsp olive oil
- 2 tsp seasoned salt
- 2 tbsp chopped rosemary

Directions:

1. Preheat air fryer to 190ºC
2. Drizzle potatoes with oil, mix in salt and rosemary
3. Place in the air fryer and cook for 20 minutes turning halfway

Yorkshire Puddings

Servings: 2
Cooking Time:xx
Ingredients:

- 1 tablespoon olive oil
- 70 g/½ cup plus ½ tablespoon plain/all-purpose flour (gluten-free if you wish)
- 100 ml/7 tablespoons milk
- 2 eggs
- salt and freshly ground black pepper

Directions:

1. You will need 4 ramekins. Preheat the air-fryer to 200ºC/400ºF.
2. Using a pastry brush, oil the base and sides of each ramekin, dividing the oil equally between the ramekins. Place the greased ramekins in the preheated air-fryer and heat for 5 minutes.
3. Meanwhile, in a food processor or using a whisk, combine the flour, milk, eggs and seasoning until you have a batter that is frothy on top. Divide the batter equally between the preheated ramekins. Return the ramekins to the air-fryer and air-fry for 20 minutes without opening the drawer. Remove the Yorkshire puddings from the ramekins and serve immediately.

Homemade Croquettes

Servings:4
Cooking Time:15 Minutes
Ingredients:

- 400 g / 14 oz white rice, uncooked
- 1 onion, sliced
- 2 cloves garlic, finely sliced
- 2 eggs, beaten
- 50 g / 3.5 oz parmesan cheese, grated
- 1 tsp salt
- 1 tsp black pepper
- 50 g / 3.5 oz breadcrumbs
- 1 tsp dried oregano

Directions:

1. In a large mixing bowl, combine the white rice, onion slices, garlic cloves slices, one beaten egg, parmesan cheese, and a sprinkle of salt and pepper.
2. Whisk the second egg in a separate bowl and place the breadcrumbs into another bowl.
3. Shape the mixture into 12 even croquettes and roll evenly in the egg, followed by the breadcrumbs.
4. Preheat the air fryer to 190 °C / 375 °F and line the bottom of the basket with parchment paper.
5. Place the croquettes in the lined air fryer basket and cook for 15 minutes, turning halfway through, until crispy and golden. Enjoy while hot as a side to your main dish.

Honey Roasted Parsnips

Servings: 4
Cooking Time:xx
Ingredients:

- 350 g/12 oz. parsnips
- 1 tablespoon plain/all-purpose flour (gluten-free if you wish)
- 1½ tablespoons runny honey
- 2 tablespoons olive oil
- salt

Directions:

1. Top and tail the parsnips, then slice lengthways, about 2 cm/¾ in. wide. Place in a saucepan with water to cover and a good pinch of salt. Bring to the boil, then boil for 5 minutes.
2. Remove and drain well, allowing any excess water to evaporate. Dust the parsnips with flour. Mix together the honey and oil in a small bowl, then toss in the parsnips to coat well in the honey and oil.
3. Preheat the air-fryer to 180ºC/350ºF.
4. Add the parsnips to the preheated air-fryer and air-fry for 14–16 minutes, depending on how dark you like the outsides (the longer you cook them, the sweeter they get).

Crispy Cinnamon French Toast

Servings:2
Cooking Time:5 Minutes
Ingredients:
- 4 slices white bread
- 4 eggs
- 200 ml milk (cow's milk, cashew milk, soy milk, or oat milk)
- 2 tbsp granulated sugar
- 1 tsp brown sugar
- 1 tsp vanilla extract
- ½ tsp ground cinnamon

Directions:
1. Preheat your air fryer to 150 °C / 300 °F and line the bottom of the basket with parchment paper.
2. Cut each of the bread slices into 2 even rectangles and set them aside.
3. In a mixing bowl, whisk together the 4 eggs, milk, granulated sugar, brown sugar, vanilla extract, and ground cinnamon.
4. Soak the bread pieces in the egg mixture until they are fully covered and soaked in the mixture.
5. Place the coated bread slices in the lined air fryer, close the lid, and cook for 4-5 minutes until the bread is crispy and golden.
6. Serve the French toast slices with whatever toppings you desire.

Sweet Potato Tots

Servings: 24
Cooking Time:xx
Ingredients:
- 2 sweet potatoes, peeled
- ½ tsp cajun seasoning
- Olive oil cooking spray
- Sea salt to taste

Directions:
1. Boil the sweet potatoes in a pan for about 15 minutes, allow to cool
2. Grate the sweet potato and mix in the cajun seasoning
3. Form into tot shaped cylinders
4. Spray the air fryer with oil, place the tots in the air fryer
5. Sprinkle with salt and cook for 8 minutes at 200ºC, turn and cook for another 8 minutes

Crispy Broccoli

Servings: 2
Cooking Time:xx
Ingredients:
- 170 g/6 oz. broccoli florets
- 2 tablespoons olive oil
- ⅛ teaspoon garlic salt
- ⅛ teaspoon freshly ground black pepper
- 2 tablespoons freshly grated Parmesan or Pecorino

Directions:
1. Preheat the air-fryer to 200ºC/400ºF.
2. Toss the broccoli in the oil, season with the garlic salt and pepper, then toss over the grated cheese and combine well. Add the broccoli to the preheated air-fryer and air-fry for 5 minutes, giving the broccoli a stir halfway through to ensure even cooking.

Desserts Recipes

New York Cheesecake

Servings: 8
Cooking Time:xx
Ingredients:

- 225g plain flour
- 100g brown sugar
- 100g butter
- 50g melted butter
- 1 tbsp vanilla essence
- 750g soft cheese
- 2 cups caster sugar
- 3 large eggs
- 50ml quark

Directions:

1. Add the flour, sugar, and 100g butter to a bowl and mix until combined. Form into biscuit shapes place in the air fryer and cook for 15 minutes at 180ºC
2. Grease a springform tin
3. Break the biscuits up and mix with the melted butter, press firmly into the tin
4. Mix the soft cheese and sugar in a bowl until creamy, add the eggs and vanilla and mix. Mix in the quark
5. Pour the cheesecake batter into the pan
6. Place in your air fryer and cook for 30 minutes at 180ºC. Leave in the air fryer for 30 minutes whilst it cools
7. Refrigerate for 6 hours

Fruit Crumble

Servings: 2
Cooking Time:xx
Ingredients:

- 1 diced apple
- 75g frozen blackberries
- 25g brown rice flour
- 2 tbsp sugar
- ½ tsp cinnamon
- 2 tbsp butter

Directions:

1. Preheat air fryer to 150ºC
2. Mix apple and blackberries in an air fryer safe baking pan
3. In a bowl mix the flour, sugar, cinnamon and butter, spoon over the fruit
4. Cook for 15 minutes

Peach Pies

Servings: 8
Cooking Time:xx
Ingredients:

- 2 peaches, peeled and chopped
- 1 tbsp lemon juice
- 3 tbsp sugar
- 1 tsp vanilla extract
- ¼ tsp salt
- 1 tsp cornstarch
- 1 pack ready made pastry
- Cooking spray

Directions:

1. Mix together peaches, lemon juice, sugar and vanilla in a bowl. Stand for 15 minutes
2. Drain the peaches keeping 1 tbsp of the liquid, mix cornstarch into the peaches
3. Cut the pastry into 8 circles, fill with the peach mix
4. Brush the edges of the pastry with water and fold over to form half moons, crimp the edges to seal
5. Coat with cooking spray
6. Add to the air fryer and cook at 170ºC for 12 minutes until golden brown

Chocolate Souffle

Servings:2
Cooking Time:15 Minutes
Ingredients:

- 2 eggs
- 4 tbsp brown sugar
- 1 tsp vanilla extract
- 4 tbsp butter, melted
- 4 tbsp milk chocolate chips
- 4 tbsp flour

Directions:

1. Preheat the air fryer to 180 °C / 350 °F. Remove the mesh basket from the machine and line it with parchment paper.
2. Separate the egg whites from the egg yolks and place them in two separate bowls.
3. Beat the yolks together with the brown sugar, vanilla extract, melted butter, milk chocolate chips, and flour in a bowl. It should form a smooth, consistent mixture.
4. Whisk the egg whites until they form stiff peaks. In batches, fold the egg whites into the chocolate mixture.
5. Divide the batter evenly between two souffle dishes and place them in the lined air fryer basket.
6. Cook the souffle dishes for 15 minutes until hot and set.

Banana Bread

Servings: 8
Cooking Time:xx
Ingredients:

- 200g flour
- 1 tsp cinnamon
- ½ tsp salt
- ¼ tsp baking soda
- 2 ripe banana mashed
- 2 large eggs
- 75g sugar
- 25g plain yogurt
- 2 tbsp oil
- 1 tsp vanilla extract
- 2 tbsp chopped walnuts
- Cooking spray

Directions:

1. Line a 6 inch cake tin with parchment paper and coat with cooking spray
2. Whisk together flour, cinnamon, salt and baking soda set aside
3. In another bowl mix together remaining ingredients, add the flour mix and combine well
4. Pour batter into the cake tin and place in the air fryer
5. Cook at 155ºC for 35 minutes turning halfway through

Sugar Dough Dippers

Servings: 12
Cooking Time:xx
Ingredients:

- 300g bread dough
- 75g melted butter
- 100g sugar
- 200ml double cream
- 200g semi sweet chocolate
- 2 tbsp amaretto

Directions:

1. Roll the dough into 2 15inch logs, cut each one into 20 slices. Cut each slice in half and twist together 2-3 times. Brush with melted butter and sprinkle with sugar
2. Preheat the air fryer to 150ºC
3. Place dough in the air fryer and cook for 5 minutes, turnover and cook for a further 3 minutes
4. Place the cream in a pan and bring to simmer over a medium heat, place the chocolate chips in a bowl and pour over the cream
5. Mix until the chocolate is melted then stir in the amaretto
6. Serve the dough dippers with the chocolate dip

Lava Cakes

Servings: 4
Cooking Time:xx

Ingredients:

- 1 ½ tbsp self raising flour
- 3 ½ tbsp sugar
- 150g butter
- 150g dark chocolate, chopped
- 2 eggs

Directions:

1. Preheat the air fryer to 175ºC
2. Grease 4 ramekin dishes
3. Melt chocolate and butter in the microwave for about 3 minutes
4. Whisk the eggs and sugar together until pale and frothy
5. Pour melted chocolate into the eggs and stir in the flour
6. Fill the ramekins ¾ full, place in the air fryer and cook for 10 minutes

Birthday Cheesecake

Servings: 8
Cooking Time:xx

Ingredients:

- 6 Digestive biscuits
- 50g melted butter
- 800g soft cheese
- 500g caster sugar
- 4 tbsp cocoa powder
- 6 eggs
- 2 tbsp honey
- 1 tbsp vanilla

Directions:

1. Flour a spring form tin to prevent sticking
2. Crush the biscuits and then mix with the melted butter, press into the bottom and sides of the tin
3. Mix the caster sugar and soft cheese with an electric mixer. Add 5 eggs, honey and vanilla. Mix well
4. Spoon half the mix into the pan and pat down well. Place in the air fryer and cook at 180ºC for 20 minutes then 160ºC for 15 minutes and then 150ºC for 20 minutes
5. Mix the cocoa and the last egg into the remaining mix. Spoon over the over the bottom layer and place in the fridge. Chill for 11 hours

Apple Fritters

Servings: 4
Cooking Time:xx

Ingredients:

- 225g self raising flour
- 200g greek yogurt
- 2 tsp sugar
- 1 tbsp cinnamon
- 1 apple peeled and chopped
- 225g icing sugar
- 2 tbsp milk

Directions:

1. Mix the flour, yogurt, sugar, cinnamon and apple together. Knead for about 3 -4 minutes
2. Mix the icing sugar and milk together to make the glaze and set aside
3. Line the air fryer with parchment paper and spray with cooking spray
4. Divide the fritter mix into four, flatten each portion and place in the air fryer
5. Cook at 185ºC for about 15 minutes turning halfway
6. Drizzle with glaze to serve

Blueberry Muffins

Servings: 12
Cooking Time:xx
Ingredients:

- 500g cups self raising flour
- 50g monk fruit
- 50g cream
- 225g oil
- 2 eggs
- 200g blueberries
- Zest and juice of 1 lemon
- 1 tbsp vanilla

Directions:

1. Mix together flour and sugar, set aside
2. In another bowl mix the remaining ingredients
3. Mix in the flour
4. Spoon the mix into silicone cupcake cases
5. Place in the air fryer and cook at 160ºC for about 10 minutes

Baked Nectarines

Servings: 4
Cooking Time:xx
Ingredients:

- 2 teaspoons maple syrup
- 1 teaspoon vanilla extract
- 1 teaspoon ground cinnamon
- 4 nectarines, halved and stones/pits removed
- chopped nuts, yogurt and runny honey, to serve (optional)

Directions:

1. Preheat the air-fryer to 180ºC/350º F.
2. Mix the maple syrup, vanilla extract and cinnamon in a ramekin or shake in a jar to combine. Lay the nectarine halves on an air-fryer liner or piece of pierced parchment paper. Drizzle over the maple syrup mix.
3. Place in the preheated air-fryer and air-fry for 9–11 minutes, until soft when pricked with a fork. Serve scattered with chopped nuts and with a generous dollop of yogurt. Drizzle over some honey if you wish.

Butter Cake

Servings: 4
Cooking Time:xx
Ingredients:

- Cooking spray
- 7 tbsp butter
- 25g white sugar
- 2 tbsp white sugar
- 1 egg
- 300g flour
- Pinch salt
- 6 tbsp milk

Directions:

1. Preheat air fryer to 175ºC
2. Spray a small fluted tube pan with cooking spray
3. Beat the butter and all of the sugar together in a bowl until creamy
4. Add the egg and mix until fluffy, add the salt and flour mix well. Add the milk and mix well
5. Put the mix in the pan and cook in the air fryer for 15 minutes

Mini Egg Buns

Servings: 8
Cooking Time:xx
Ingredients:

- 100g self raising flour
- 100g caster sugar
- 100g butter
- 2 eggs
- 2 tbsp honey
- 1 tbsp vanilla essence
- 300g soft cheese
- 100g icing sugar
- 2 packets of Mini Eggs

Directions:

1. Cream the butter and sugar together until light and fluffy, beat in the eggs one at a time
2. Add the honey and vanilla essence, fold in the flour a bit at a time
3. Divide the mix into 8 bun cases and place in the air fryer. Cook at 180ºC for about 20 minutes
4. Cream the soft cheese and icing sugar together to make the topping
5. Allow the buns to cool, pipe on the topping mix and add mini eggs

White Chocolate Pudding

Servings:2
Cooking Time:15 Minutes
Ingredients:

- 100 g / 3.5 oz white chocolate
- 50 g brown sugar
- 2 tbsp olive oil
- ½ tsp vanilla extract
- 4 egg whites, plus two egg yolks

Directions:

1. Preheat the air fryer to 180 °C / 350 °F and line the mesh basket with parchment paper or grease it with olive oil.
2. Place the white chocolate in a saucepan and place it over low heat until it melts, being careful not to let the chocolate burn.
3. Stir in the brown sugar, olive oil, and vanilla extract.
4. Whisk the egg whites and egg yolks in a bowl until well combined. Fold a third of the eggs into the white chocolate mixture and stir until it forms a smooth and consistent mixture. Repeat twice more with the other two-thirds of the eggs.
5. Pour the white chocolate pudding mixture evenly into two ramekins and place the ramekins in the lined air fryer basket. Cook for 15 minutes until the pudding is hot and set on top.

Chocolate Orange Fondant

Servings: 4
Cooking Time:xx
Ingredients:

- 2 tbsp self raising flour
- 4 tbsp caster sugar
- 115g dark chocolate
- 115g butter
- 1 medium orange rind and juice
- 2 eggs

Directions:

1. Preheat the air fryer to 180ºC and grease 4 ramekins
2. Place the chocolate and butter in a glass dish and melt over a pan of hot water, stir until the texture is creamy
3. Beat the eggs and sugar together until pale and fluffy
4. Add the orange and egg mix to the chocolate and mix
5. Stir in the flour until fully mixed together
6. Put the mix into the ramekins, place in the air fryer and cook for 12 minutes. Leave to stand for 2 minutes before serving

Lemon Buns

Servings: 12
Cooking Time:xx

Ingredients:

- 100g butter
- 100g caster sugar
- 2 eggs
- 100g self raising flour
- ½ tsp vanilla essence
- 1 tsp cherries
- 50g butter
- 100g icing sugar
- ½ small lemon rind and juice

Directions:

1. Preheat the air fryer to 170ºC
2. Cream the 100g butter, sugar and vanilla together until light and fluffy
3. Beat in the eggs one at a time adding a little flour with each
4. Fold in the remaining flour
5. Half fill bun cases with the mix, place in the air fryer and cook for 8 minutes
6. Cream 50g butter then mix in the icing sugar, stir in the lemon
7. Slice the top off each bun and create a butterfly shape using the icing to hold together. Add a 1/3 cherry to each one

Peanut Butter & Chocolate Baked Oats

Servings:9
Cooking Time:xx

Ingredients:

- 150 g/1 heaped cup rolled oats/quick-cooking oats
- 50 g/⅓ cup dark chocolate chips or buttons
- 300 ml/1¼ cups milk or plant-based milk
- 50 g/3½ tablespoons Greek or plant-based yogurt
- 1 tablespoon runny honey or maple syrup
- ½ teaspoon ground cinnamon or ground ginger
- 65 g/scant ⅓ cup smooth peanut butter

Directions:

1. Stir all the ingredients together in a bowl, then transfer to a baking dish that fits your air-fryer drawer.
2. Preheat the air-fryer to 180ºC/350ºF.
3. Add the baking dish to the preheated air-fryer and air-fry for 10 minutes. Remove from the air-fryer and serve hot, cut into 9 squares.

Zebra Cake

Servings: 6
Cooking Time:xx
Ingredients:

- 115g butter
- 2 eggs
- 100g caster sugar
- 1 tbsp cocoa powder
- 100g self raising flour
- 30ml milk
- 1tsp vanilla

Directions:

1. Preheat air fryer to 160ºC
2. Line a 6 inch baking tin
3. Beat together the butter and sugar until light and fluffy
4. Add eggs one at a time then add the vanilla and milk
5. Add the flour and mix well
6. Divide the mix in half
7. Add cocoa powder to half the mix and mix well
8. Add a scoop of each of the batters at a time until it's all in the tin, place in the air fryer and cook for 30 minutes

S'mores

Servings: 2
Cooking Time:xx
Ingredients:

- 2 graham crackers, broken in half
- 2 marshmallows, halved
- 2 pieces of chocolate

Directions:

1. Place 2 halves of graham crackers in the air fryer and add a marshmallow to each sticky side down
2. Cook in the air fryer at 180ºC for 5 minutes until the marshmallows are golden
3. Remove from the air fryer add a piece of chocolate and top with the other half of graham crackers

Chocolate-glazed Banana Slices

Servings:2
Cooking Time:10 Minutes
Ingredients:

- 2 bananas
- 1 tbsp honey
- 1 tbsp chocolate spread, melted
- 2 tbsp milk chocolate chips

Directions:

1. Preheat the air fryer to 180 °C / 350 °F. Remove the mesh basket from the machine and line it with parchment paper.
2. Cut the two bananas into even slices and place them in the lined air fryer basket.
3. In a small bowl, mix the honey and melted chocolate spread. Use a brush to glaze the banana slices. Carefully press the milk chocolate chips into the banana slices enough so that they won't fall out when you transfer the bananas into the air fryer.
4. Carefully slide the mesh basket into the air fryer, close the lid, and cook for 10 minutes until the bananas are hot and the choc chips have melted.
5. Enjoy the banana slices on their own or with a side of ice cream.

Cherry Pies

Servings: 6

Cooking Time:xx

Ingredients:

- 300g prepared shortcrust pastry
- 75g cherry pie filling
- Cooking spray
- 3 tbsp icing sugar
- ½ tsp milk

Directions:

1. Cut out 6 pies with a cookie cutter
2. Add 1 ½ tbsp filling to each pie
3. Fold the dough in half and seal around the edges with a fork
4. Place in the air fryer, spray with cooking spray
5. Cook at 175ºC for 10 minutes
6. Mix icing sugar and milk and drizzled over cooled pies to serve

Lemon Pies

Servings: 6

Cooking Time:xx

Ingredients:

- 1 pack of pastry
- 1 egg beaten
- 200g lemon curd
- 225g powdered sugar
- ½ lemon

Directions:

1. Preheat the air fryer to 180ºC
2. Cut out 6 circles from the pastry using a cookie cutter
3. Add 1 tbsp of lemon curd to each circle, brush the edges with egg and fold over
4. Press around the edges of the dough with a fork to seal
5. Brush the pies with the egg and cook in the air fryer for 10 minutes
6. Mix the lemon juice with the powdered sugar to make the icing and drizzle on the cooked pies

Appendix : Recipes Index

Cauliflower With Hot Sauce And Blue Cheese Sauce 62
Celery Root Fries 65
Cheese Scones 11
Cheese Wontons 16
Cheeseburger Egg Rolls 38
Cheesy Garlic Asparagus 61
Cheesy Meatball Sub 34
Cheesy Taco Crescents 14
Cherry Pies 76
Chicken & Potatoes 28
Chicken And Cheese Chimichangas 32
Chicken Balls, Greek-style 23
Chicken Kiev 27
Chicken Tikka 24
Chickpea And Sweetcorn Falafel 56
Chinese Chilli Beef 42
Chinese Pork With Pineapple 38
Chocolate Orange Fondant 73
Chocolate Souffle 69
Chocolate-glazed Banana Slices 75
Cod In Parma Ham 46
Copycat Fish Fingers 44
Corn Nuts 15
Corn On The Cob 63
Courgette Burgers 53
Crispy Broccoli 67
Crispy Cinnamon French Toast 67
Crispy Cornish Hen 33
Crispy Nacho Prawns 50
Crunchy Chicken Tenders 27
Crunchy Fish 47
Cumin Shoestring Carrots 12

E

Easy Cheesy Scrambled Eggs 6
Egg & Bacon Breakfast Cups 10
Extra Crispy Popcorn Shrimp 44

F

Fish In Parchment Paper 48
Fish Sticks With Tartar Sauce Batter 43
Flat Mushroom Pizzas 54
French Toast 12
Fruit Crumble 68

G

Garlic Tilapia 48
Garlic-parsley Prawns 50

Gluten Free Honey And Garlic Shrimp 50
Grain-free Chicken Katsu 31

H

Halloumi Fries 13
Hamburgers 36
Healthy Stuffed Peppers 11
Homemade Croquettes 66
Honey Cajun Chicken Thighs 33
Honey Roasted Parsnips 66

I

Italian Meatballs 40
Italian Rice Balls 20

J

Jalapeño Pockets 19
Jalapeño Poppers 22
Japanese Pork Chops 42

L

Lava Cakes 71
Lemon Buns 74
Lemon Pies 76

M

Mac & Cheese Bites 18
Mexican Rice 63
Mini Egg Buns 73
Mini Quiche 54
Miso Mushrooms On Sourdough Toast 55
Mongolian Beef 39
Monte Cristo Breakfast Sandwich 7
Morning Sausage Wraps 10
Mozzarella Sticks 17
Mustard Glazed Pork 36

N

Nashville Chicken 30
New York Cheesecake 68

O

Olive Stained Turkey Breast 29
Onion Pakoda 19

Onion Rings 60
Oozing Baked Eggs 7

P

Paneer Tikka 57
Pao De Queijo 16
Parmesan-coated Fish Fingers 49
Pasta Chips 15
Peach Pies 69
Peanut Butter & Chocolate Baked Oats 74
Pepper & Lemon Chicken Wings 30
Pepperoni Bread 14
Peppery Lemon Shrimp 45
Pesto Salmon 43
Pizza Chicken Nuggets 32
Plantain Fries 12
Polenta Fries 6
Pork Chilli Cheese Dogs 42
Pork Jerky 19
Pork With Chinese 5 Spice 36
Potato Hay 64
Potato Wedges With Rosemary 65
Pretzel Bites 20
Pumpkin Fries 64

R

Ranch Style Fish Fillets 48
Raspberry Breakfast Pockets 8
Ratatouille 59
Ravioli Air Fryer Style 59
Roasted Almonds 22
Roasted Garlic 52
Roasted Vegetable Pasta 52

S

S'mores 75
Salmon Patties 43
Salt And Vinegar Chickpeas 16
Shrimp Wrapped With Bacon 45
Snack Style Falafel 21
Southern Style Pork Chops 39
Spicy Chicken Wing Drummettes 25
Spicy Chickpeas 18
Spicy Green Beans 63
Spinach And Egg Air Fryer Breakfast Muffins 58
Spring Ratatouille 52
Spring Rolls 17
Steak Popcorn Bites 35

Sticky Chicken Tikka Drumsticks 24
Stuffed Jacket Potatoes 60
Sugar Dough Dippers 70
Swede Fries 7
Sweet Potato Fries 8
Sweet Potato Taquitos 56
Sweet Potato Tots 67
Sweet Potato Wedges 64

T

Tangy Breakfast Hash 13
Tender Ham Steaks 35
Thai-style Tuna Fishcakes 47
Tilapia Fillets 46
Toad In The Hole, Breakfast Style 9
Tortellini Bites 18
Turkey And Mushroom Burgers 26
Turkey Cutlets In Mushroom Sauce 31

V

Vegan Fried Ravioli 51
Vegan Meatballs 51
Veggie Bakes 55

W

White Chocolate Pudding 73
Whole Sweet Potatoes 61

Y

Yorkshire Puddings 65

Z

Zebra Cake 75
Zingy Roasted Carrots 62

Printed in Great Britain
by Amazon

36986598R00051